WHAT DO YOU DARE TO DREAM?
www.idaretodreamproject.com

Valerie Jeannis has created a wake up call to action with her book, Dare to Dream: A Dreamer's Manifesto. Having Valerie visit your school or campus will only inspire others and equip them with a guide on how to move forward and overcome the obstacles of self-doubt and fear so their dreams can become a reality. I highly recommend Valerie, her books and her presentations.

JEWELS MULLER, MA, Founder and CEO of Chicks Connect, Inc.

Dare to Dream is the prime inspiration that is needed in all communities. You will be challenged to stand against all odds even when others do not understand the poignancy of your dream. If anyone ever doubt themselves in anything, *Dare to Dream* will serve as a catalyst to motivate and to reawaken the hidden purpose that might be laying dormant inside of you.

DR. RUBEN C. BEAUBRUN, James M. Kieran Junior High School

Valerie is empowering women to push beyond boundaries, rejection and fear; without apologizing or compromising. She is a talented, inspirational and a beautiful reminder that all dreams matter and can come true with passion, perseverance and execution!

NICOLE VIETOR, COO Jack Travis Logistics

Valerie's Dare to Dream message is simple, powerful, and very useful. A valuable read for those who are ready to dare to take the necessary leap of faith usually required when one pursues his or her dreams.

ALLYN REID, Co-Founder of Secret Knock &
Co-Founder of Sherpa Press

Dare to Dream is GREAT! The piece about being an "extraordinary failure" was fantastic. Valerie not only gives people permission to fail, but encourages it through her examples and metaphors. Two thumbs up!!

KEN COURTRIGHT, Founder of Today's Growth Consultant

Once again Ms. Valerie Jeannis amazes her readers with an in-depth, soul searching journey to self-discovery and actualization. Her writing is both illuminating and affirming, as it assist the reader in acknowledging their God given gifts, and then with great insight and witty turn of phrase, guides in turning their dreams into reality. This is truly a must read!

REV. DR. BISHOP CARLTON T BROWN, Senior Pastor
Bethel Gospel Assembly, Harlem, NY

Dare to Dream is one of the rare books written through the lens of someone who has actually dared to dream, then dared to challenge themselves and others to actualize those dream into reality! The same way Valerie is taking action and bringing dreams to life, this book and Valerie's programs can do exactly that for you!

DR. JEFFREY MAGEE, Publisher, Performance/P360 Magazine

The late great Roger Anthony said, *"It's one thing to teach a principle and another to live it, but the greatest by far is to so thoroughly be it that your very presence does the teaching."* Valerie Jeannis so thoroughly lives her "Dare to Dream" principles that her words will speak to you from deep within, helping you step more boldly into your own dreams.

DAVE AUSTIN, Founder of Extreme Focus
Author of the International Bestselling Book

Valerie Jeannis is a provoking voice for this generation. She is a doer and through Dare to Dream she invites and challenges readers to live their dreams by taking intentional actions. She is an accomplished overcomer who has earned the right to share these effective principles because she dared to dream her own dream and you can too! A must read for the faith leaper who is ready to make life happen.

DR. ANNA MCCOY, Chief Global Officer, UrbanAmerica

I LOVED this book! We all have big dreams but do we have what it takes to turn them into reality? In this fascinating and inspiring book, Valerie shows us what it takes to give birth to the dream and the dreamer in all of us. She shares her own struggles and victories in such a candid and honest way that you can't help but feel compelled to go for your dream as well.

I am so grateful to hold this book in my hands, the beautiful result of a dreamer who refused to quit on her dreams, and inspires us not to quit on ours as well.

PAULINE KERKHOFF, International Bestselling Author

Wow, Valerie, what a great ride! As I read Dare to Dream, I really felt like I got to know you, your process, AND was being supported, motivated, and reminded of all the things that I would say to a client as their coach. Thank you for coaching me. You have something VERY powerful here.

DR. REV. ROBERT B. JAMES, President, One Sphera, Inc.

I have witnessed firsthand Valerie Jeannis' relentless determination in using the principles within this book. It is because of that determination and conviction that she refused to let her dream die and the reason why the lives of many will be impacted with the Dare to Dream message.

JOAN BYRD, High School for Environmental Studies

Valerie Jeannis is a gifted author and thinker. Through her writing, the intentional lifestyle habits of reflection, process and implementation, she has left a blueprint for others to follow. I highly recommend this book to any person whom desires to courageously confront the truth within themselves, re-write their history and defy the boundaries of doubt and unbelief in their pursuit of the extraordinary.

REV. EBONY S. SMALL Associate Minister, Bethel Gospel Assembly

Whether you're at the beginning of your journey or you've been at it for a while, Dare to Dream has something for everyone. It's the perfect catalyst to help you go all the way.

AARON YOUNG, Chairman & CEO at Laughlin Associates, Inc.

Inspirational. Practical. Heartfelt. Dare to Dream is perfect! It is a brilliant guide that inspires you to dream again and gives you practical insights and wisdom to keep your dream alive and thriving. If you have a dream or want to reconnect to your dreams, Dare to Dream will show you the way. Well done Valerie!

RADIAH RHODES, CEO, evókLife
Global Design Program Manager, COVERGIRL Cosmetics

WOW! What a beautiful, well written manifesto! Valerie really lays out the steps oh HOW to make your dream happen. Full of great motivating reminders of just how great we are, and how important achieving your dreams are - not just for you, but for the world around you. I dare you to dream! Don't know how to get started? Read Dare to Dream!

SEPTEMBER DOHRMANN, President & CEO
of CEO Space International

WRITE A REVIEW
READ THE BOOK & SHARE YOUR THOUGHTS & TAKEAWAYS.

POST THE REVIEWS ON AMAZON AT
bit.ly/D2DMANIFESTO.

POST PICTURES OF DARE TO DREAM. TAG WITH #DaretoDreamBook   #IDaretoDreamProject SO WE CAN FIND YOU AND SHOW YOU SOME LOVE.

UNAPOLOGETIC PRESS
55 West 116th Street, PO Box 360
New York, NY 10026
Phone: 347.871.3246
Email: info@unapologeticpress.com

Dare to Dream Books are available at special discounts when purchased in quantity for premiums and promotions as well as fundraising or educational use. Special editions can also be created to specification. For details, contact **info@unapologeticpress.com** or the address above.

INTERIOR LAYOUT & DESIGN: Unapologetic Press
AUTHOR'S PHOTO: Soulscaping Photography

ISBN 978-1-945106-00-2 paperback
ISBN 978-1-945106-01-9 hardcover
**Copyright © 2015 by Valerie Jeannis. All rights reserved.
Printed in the United States of America.**

Library of Congress Cataloging-in-Publication Data
is on file at the Library of Congress

No part of this book may be reproduced or transmitted in any form or by any means, mechanical or electric, including photocopying and recording, or by any information storage and retrieval system, without permission in writing from author or publisher. Please direct your inquires to **info@unapologeticpress.com**.

A DREAMER'S MANIFESTO*

*(*bold, sometimes rebellious, call to action*)*

DARE TO DREAM

VALERIE JEANNIS

UNAPOLOGETIC PRESS

to Johane Francois and Eileen Margret Woodburn

WE ARE THE ONES WHO DARE

THE FUN. THE FEARLESS. THE PURPOSE-DRIVEN. **THE UNAPOLOGETIC.** We want more than the lives that we are living and we are doing something about it. WE ACCEPT THE ALMOST CERTAIN REALITY THAT WE WILL BE TALKED ABOUT, MISUNDERSTOOD AND REJECTED. **WE TAKE DRASTIC MEASURES TO MAKE OUR DREAMS HAPPEN AND WILLINGLY WALK THE ROAD LESS TRAVELED.** WE CHOOSE DAILY TO CARE LESS ABOUT PEOPLE'S OPINIONS AND BREAK UP WITH FEAR. **WE ARE RELENTLESS.** UNQUENCHABLE DREAMERS. **EXTRAORDINARY FAILURES.** WE ARE A COMMUNITY. **WE CELEBRATE, SUPPORT AND ENCOURAGE EACH OTHER.** WE GO FOR GREAT. **WE OWN OUR EXTRAORDINARY.** WE DARE TO DREAM AND DARE TO PURSUE OUR DREAMS **UNAPOLOGETICALLY.** AND WE HAVE FUN ALONG THE WAY. #iDaretoDreamProject

www.iDaretoDreamProject.com

CONTENTS

9   Manifesto
13   Introduction

1. DARE TO DREAM

21   It Starts with a Dream
26   How to Dare to Dream
29   Dare to Dream
38   How to Not Be a Delusional Dreamer
41   Follow the Trails
48   How to Find Your Dream
51   Conception of a Dream

2. BREAK UP WITH FEAR

59   Monsters Under the Bed
64   How to Break Up with Fear
67   Someone Else Said So
75   I Can't Do This
80   How to Be an Extraordinary Failure
81   A Mindset Issue
87   The Cost of No
93   A Second Chance
98   How to Dream a New Dream

3. DARE TO PURSUE

- 103 The Cost of Yes
- 111 How to Overcome Decision Paralysis
- 113 Go for Great
- 118 How to Maintain a Standard of Excellence
- 119 A Part of the Process
- 127 Essential Connections

4. BIRTH YOUR DREAM

- 137 Any Minute Now
- 147 The State of Constipation
- 154 How to Get Back to a State of Flow
- 157 Behind Closed Doors
- 163 Unquenchable

THE APPENDIX

- 171 Acknowledgements
- 177 Dreamer's Dictionary
- 184 About the Author
- 187 Notes

WHEN IT'S ALL SAID AND DONE, YOU WILL NEVER HAVE TO WONDER, **"WHAT IF I TRIED?"**

INTRODUCTION
NO WHAT-IFS

I had a conversation with God and I asked Him,
Who should I write this book to?

He responded,
Write this book to the fun, the fearless, the purpose-driven,
The ones who want more than the lives that they're living and are prepared to do something about it,
The ones who are willing to accept the almost certain reality that they will be talked about, misunderstood, and rejected.

God, what should I tell them?

Let them know about the necessity of a dream, the price of the pursuit, the price of aborting the dream.

Write this book to the unquenchable dreamers,
The relentless ones,
The misunderstood ones,
The tired dreamers and the ones just starting out.
Let them know they are not alone.
Remind them it's possible.

Remind them they can do this.

*Write this book to those who dare to dream
    and pursue their dreams
And tell them to keep moving forward no
    matter what.*

But God, what if ...

You got this.
Valerie Jeannis, The Assignment, 2015

Sometimes I ask myself, *if you knew that this is what it would take to make your dreams a reality, would you have still said yes?*

I would love to say that my answer would be, absolutely, but sometimes, I just don't know.

It all started with a bucket list and an idea to travel to all fifty states interviewing women and filming a documentary of the journey. But then, it evolved.

For as long as I can remember, my passion has been women empowerment. It's what led me to start a mentorship group for young girls. It's what led me to pursue a Master of Social Work degree. And in 2010, it's what inspired the *I Dare to Dream Project*, a campaign daring women and youth to pursue their dreams unapologetically.

My dream became to create a platform where women can be inspired, challenged and equipped to pursue their dreams. A platform where their voices can be heard and their dreams shared; where those who dare to dream can be showcased and celebrated. A platform where we bring back the message "it's possible" and remind others and ourselves that regardless where we're starting from, our dreams can become a reality.

I learned though, as exciting as dreams are, they come at a cost. They require so much of you – so much creativity, so much determination and so much persistence – so much of not just part of you, but all of you. My dream went beyond who I was and placed the greatest demand on my faith in God, myself, others, and the dream itself. But I was determined. I knew what I wanted; I believed it was possible; and I made up my mind to go after it.

For years I talked about the campaign and road trip. Finally, in 2013, it was happening. However, just as I was getting ready to hit the road, I was told that I was not ready. Since "they" were the experts and I was "just a girl with a dream" with little to no experience, little to no money, and little to no following, I took their word for it and placed everything on hold indefinitely. Looking back, I don't know if I made the right decision, but it was the choice I made and it wasn't an easy one to accept because of how far along I was in the process. The website was launched; interviewees were contacted; announcements were made and goodbyes were said. I was so convinced I was going to be on the road that I turned down once-in-a-lifetime opportunities, like being a part of my brother's wedding party.

I felt like such a failure. I was angry, disappointed, confused and embarrassed. I was so frustrated with God because I couldn't understand why He would give me this dream, yet allow so many roadblocks. I was ready to throw my hands up and put my dreams to rest. But, **there's something about a dream that refuses to die**. I didn't know how; I just knew I had to keep pursuing.

HERE'S TO YOU

Dare to Dream started out as life support for a dying dream and a tired dreamer. It was a conversation between God and myself that is now a message to all those with a dream that compels them to say yes.

No, it's not easy and yes, there is a cost. But when it's all said and done, you will never have to wonder, *"What if I tried?"* Instead, you will talk about the years you dared to dream and pursue, and will share the stories of what happened after you said yes to your dreams.

So here's to you –
The crazy one,
the extraordinary one,
The dreamer in pursuit.
Be unapologetic.
Be unreasonable.
Be wise.
Be unquenchable.
Dare to dream and go for great.
And Live.
Live Fearlessly.
Live on Purpose.
Live without Apology.
Just Live.

from one unquenchable dreamer to another.

THE DOCUMENTARY

WHAT DO YOU DARE TO DREAM?

SUBMIT A VIDEO SHARING YOUR DREAM AND BE A PART OF THE DOCUMENTARY

FOLLOW US ON [f] [◎] [▶] @idaretodreamproject

REFUSE TO ALLOW YOUR CIRCUMSTANCES TO DICTATE WHAT IS POSSIBLE FOR YOUR LIFE.

IT MATTERS
IT STARTS WITH A DREAM

I was once asked, *"Does a dream even matter?"*

In a time when people are satisfied to just make it through the day or when many aren't even pursuing their dreams, but seem to be doing ok, does a dream even matter?

Absolutely, without a doubt - *YES*.

Dreams matter.

When we dream, we have an opportunity to create the world, our world, the way we want it to be instead of simply accepting things as they are or letting whatever happens happen.

There was a time when my dream and my sincere prayer to God was for a Section 8 *government subsidized* apartment in a nice neighborhood, because in my mind that was a step up from "the projects", *public housing*, where I was living. There was a time when I sat my mom and stepdad down with my then fiancé beside me and explained to them that I didn't need to go to college because I already knew what I was going to do with my life – I was going to be a supportive wife and work with my husband as he traveled as a preacher. There was a time when I made up my mind that I wouldn't go anywhere a car couldn't take me because I was afraid of dying in the air or drowning in the middle of the ocean.

For years, my life and aspirations were dictated by what I saw in my environment and what people saw for me, until the day I found the courage to call off my wedding and end that relationship, a story I share in my first book.

While dealing with the aftermath of the breakup, instead of going to class, I spent most of my days that year in bed and under the covers because I felt lost. I built all my plans around that relationship. Now that I was single again for the first time in over four years, I didn't know what was next for me.

One night, in the midst of my desperation, I stood at my window and, looking up to heaven, I prayed, *"God, there has to be more to life than this. There has to be more than the life I'm living."*

A few weeks later, while in my junior year in college, I was presented with an opportunity to study abroad in Paris, France.

Have you ever been so desperate that you were willing to face your biggest fears in order to make a change?

As much as I was afraid of getting on a plane, the life that I was living was no longer an option for me. So I decided to put my degree on hold, resign from my job, step down from every leadership position I occupied and with tears in my eyes kiss my mother goodbye. While walking down the surprisingly empty corridors of JFK airport toward the gate of my flight, I learned something I strive to remind myself of every time I'm confronted with something that scares me – **there is life on the other side of fear.**

After an eight-hour flight the plane landed and there I was, a girl from the projects in Harlem, living and studying abroad in Paris! It was that trip, on the other side of the world, in a place I had never been, among people I did not know, who spoke a language I did not fully speak, that taught me the key to daring to dream – refuse to allow your circumstances to dictate what's possible for your life.

IT'S POSSIBLE

There are so many things we want that we convince ourselves is not possible because of our circumstances. What if it has nothing to do with where you are or what you have? **What if the truth is, you're just scared or just too comfortable to either make a change or go after what you claim you want?**

No one could have convinced me that Paris would have been a part of my story and there was nothing in my or my mother's bank account that even suggested it would be possible for me to live abroad for a year. Yet, there I was, simply because I was in a place in my life where I was so desperate for change that I was willing to break up with fear and take a leap of faith.

During one of my two trips back home that year, I remember sitting in the window seat of the plane and looking at the lights from the houses below. As I watched the landscape, I prayed, *"God, even the biggest house is just a box from up here. Since it's all the same to You, I would like a big box too please."*

No longer was I praying for a section 8 apartment. What I really wanted was to own my own brownstone or townhouse because I realized that **even if I didn't know how it would happen, it was possible.**

DOES A DREAM EVEN MATTER?

When I was asked, "*Does a dream even matter?*," these are the thoughts that immediately came to mind. Had it not been for a **dream***, *a vision that you could be, do, have or create something that exists first in your heart and mind only,* I would've accepted marrying someone who did not have my best interest at heart. Had it not been for a dream, I would've accepted a life defined by others and my circumstances. Had it not been for a dream, there wouldn't have even been a plane for me to be afraid of!

It took desperation and an immense dissatisfaction with the life I was living to bring me to a place where, for the first time, without the influence of anyone I knew or anyone who thought they knew me, I asked and answered two life-changing questions that I now challenge you to answer – *What do you want? And who do you want to be?*

We have to learn to dream, not based on what we have, but instead based on what's possible. And truly, anything *is* possible. You have to develop an attitude that in the face of doubt confidently responds, "*Why not and why not me?*"

Does a dream even matter? Absolutely yes, because it is through our dreams we find a sense of purpose, direction, and self-worth. Dreams change lives, both ours and the life of others.

Dreams don't care who you are, what people think about you, or where you are starting. Dreams don't care about how many times you may have failed or gotten it wrong in the past and they don't discriminate. Dreams are ours, if we want them. They have no limits and they go across all borders. No one can tell you that your dream is wrong or that it's not possible, because **dreams are the places where we fly**. So spread your wings.

We all have the ability to dream and beyond that, we all have the right to dream. The question is, *will you dare to dream? And if so, what do you dare to dream?*

HOW TO DARE TO DREAM

> **dare to dream**
> to imagine that you can be, do, have, or create something that exists first in your heart and mind only and that may defy your present circumstances

1. **DETERMINE WHAT YOU WANT.** Not what others want for you. Not what you think you can get based on what you have and where you are. But what *you* really truly want.

2. **BE UNAPOLOGETIC.** Make no apologies for your dreams and your willingness to boldly pursue it.

3. **DON'T BE A DELUSIONAL DREAMER.** Know what it takes and be prepared to do what it takes to make your dreams a reality.

4. **BREAK UP WITH FEAR.** Refuse to allow fear to keep you from going after what you want.

5. **BE AN EXTRAORDINARY FAILURE.** Embrace the possibility of failure knowing that it's a part of the process. Learn and keep moving forward.

6. **MAKE DECISIONS NOT EXCUSES.** We all have challenges. Don't allow yours to stop you. Make them work for you.

7. **GO FOR GREAT.** Don't simply rest on your talents and abilities. Choose greatness. Give your best to the pursuit, holding nothing back.

8. **TAKE DRASTIC MEASURES.** Instead of just waiting for things to happen, use unconventional, out-of-the-box methods to make your dreams a reality.

9. **K.I.S.S. YOUR DREAMS.** Keep It Super Simple. Don't make things complicated when they don't have to be.

10. **BE UNQUENCHABLE.** Make up your mind that no matter what, you will finish and go all the way.

THIS IS AN OPPORTUNITY TO **DREAM ABOUT CREATING THINGS THE WAY YOU WANT THEM TO BE** INSTEAD OF ACCEPTING THEM THE WAY THEY ARE.

UNAPOLOGETIC
DARE TO DREAM

I will never forget the day I was told I would get to take seven members of my family to Disney World. It was August 2009. I was twenty-four and in Scottsdale, Arizona attending my first personal development conference, Breakthrough to Success (BTS) with Jack Canfield, co-creator of the Chicken Soup for the Soul book series. During one of our sessions, Jack shared a story about how Lou Holtz, the famous Notre Dame football coach, had his bucket list turned into a large bulletin and placed right next to the door of the locker room. One day after a meeting, someone was walking out of the locker room when they saw his list and told him they can help him accomplish one of his goals.

As I sat there listening to Lou's story, I took the time to look around the room full of CEOs, entrepreneurs and people who were the top in their fields. I realized that if I was ever going to share my bucket list, this would be the room to share it in. At the time, I didn't have a list, but that didn't stop me from asking Jack if I could share my non-existent list with the other 300 attendees. To my surprise, I was told yes!

That night, I stayed up for hours creating my bucket list and putting as many specific things as I could think of on a regular 8.5 x 11 sheet of paper.

True to their word, on the last day of the conference, the staff distributed my makeshift bucket list pamphlet and when everyone walked in, Valerie was on their seats.

As I was walking across the room, this man, who I never saw before, tapped me on the shoulder and said, "I can do this for you."

One of the things on my list was I wanted to travel to Disney world with seven members of my family and stay at a five-star hotel.

He said, "I don't have a five-star hotel, but I can do this for you."

It took some time for what he was saying to fully register. Then he asked me, "What do you want?"

"I want to go to Disney world with seven members of my family."

"You already have that. What else do you want?"

I stood there trying to figure out whether or not he was serious and in the end decided to just go with it.

"I want eight round trip plane tickets."

"Ok, what else do you want?"

"A Disney ticket for everyday we're there."

"Ok, what else do you want?"

At that point, I responded, "What?! There's more?!" To which he responded, "If you don't know what you want, then don't ask!"

I immediately responded, "Wait, we need food!"

He looked at me, nodded and asked, "When do you want to go?"

I was starting graduate school in two weeks and the main thought going through my mind was, *if I say next year, what are the chances that I will get this trip?*

"Next week."

Once again he looked at me, nodded, pulled out his phone, dialed a number and asked whoever picked up, "Is the house available?" Turns out, it was. All I had to do was email him a list with the names of everyone that was going. That's when I realized he was serious.

One week later, my family and I were in Orlando, Florida, experiencing Disney World and staying at this beautiful 7-bedroom summer rental house in a gated community. In return, *all* this man wanted was that I never share with anyone who he was. That's it!

Once again I found myself in a place that, according to my circumstances and resources, I should have never been, yet there I was.

My year abroad in Paris taught me how to dream. The bucket list and trip to Disney World proved to me that the impossible was possible and that dreams really can and do come true. I was just a girl who, in a moment of desperation, took a leap of faith and said yes when presented with the opportunity to study abroad. That same opportunity was made available to every single student in my class that day and several other classes. The only difference between those of us who went and those who didn't was that one group said yes and followed through.

It was the same thing with Disney World, except, this time, instead of someone giving me an opportunity, I created one. I had an idea, made a request and got a yes. Then, I followed through by creating the bucket list, making all the necessary copies, and then giving them to the staff.

Our journeys won't all be the same. We won't all face the same challenges or even want the same things.

But whatever you want to be, do, have or create is possible. And it's possible for you. The question is, *what do you want?*

WHAT DO YOU WANT?

It's a fairly simple question, but one that many of us have a hard time answering. In our minds, *"What do you want?"* somehow gets converted to, *"Based on what I have, where I am, what people think about me, and what I've seen those around me accomplish, what do I think I can get?"* And so we settle, while keeping our true dreams and desires hidden in our hearts.

But you can change that by **daring to dream***, *to imagine that you can be, do, have, or create something that exists first in your heart and mind only and that may defy your present circumstances.* Refuse to allow where you are to limit the magnitude of your dream, whether you decide you want to do something big or something small. And dream with no shame, no regret, and no apology for wanting what you want.

That kind of audacity and boldness will make some people around you very uncomfortable, especially those who aren't living their dreams. Some will have an attitude that says, *"Who are you to think that you can do this?"* Others will give you their opinions about what your dream should look or what would be more "acceptable".

ACCELERATORS AND ANCHORS

When it comes to sharing your dream, you will generally encounter three main types of people – accelerators, anchors, and those who could care less. Our focus will be on the first two.

Accelerators* are *the people with contagious faith that make you feel like you can do anything*. They are the cheerleaders. You're excited and they're excited with and for you. Their encouragement and feedback fuels your momentum. On the other hand, **anchors*** are like brakes on a car. While they may be excited for you, they will, more often than not, see and point out all potential pitfalls and dangers before they celebrate or cheer you on. Their responses are more practical and sobering and can at times feed your fears and insecurities.

I was at a conference when I first got the idea that inspired the *I Dare to Dream Project*. I was so excited that I shared it with the person sitting next to me, and the first thing she said was, *"That's a great idea, but you don't have any money."* Anchor.

How she came to that conclusion, I have no idea, but I was immediately deflated. The voices in my head agreed with her and started saying, *"Yeah, it's true Valerie, you don't have any money."* And just that quickly, I gave in to doubt, which delayed me from going after my dream for years.

That was not the first, nor the last time I shared a dream, idea or even a win with someone who turned out to be an anchor when what I was looking for was an accelerator.

Both anchors and accelerators are important and each serve their own unique purposes. You simply have to know who is who and engage the right person at the right time, because some people are simply not in a position to fuel your advancement with positivity and encouragement. And if that's what you're looking for and if you're not grounded in your faith and confidence, the wrong reaction may cause you to lose your passion and even abort your dream. The challenge is you will usually discover who is who after you've shared with someone and experienced their reaction.

YOUR DREAM WILL BE CHALLENGED

I'm going to tell you upfront that both you and your dream will be challenged countless times throughout this journey, both by external forces – *circumstances, people, finances, etc.* – and internal forces – *negative self-talk, fear, doubt, lack of confidence, etc.* It's a part of the process, so you have to be prepared to stand for your dream.

1. **UNDERSTAND YOUR ROLE AND RESPONSIBILITY.** Once you have a dream inside of you, that makes you a dreamer, a visionary, a leader. Your status changes, which also brings a change in responsibilities. It is now your job to nurture, protect and develop that dream, because it is a gift and privilege that is entrusted to you to bring into the world.

2. **MAKE A NO-MATTER-WHAT DECISION*,** *deciding from the beginning what the end will be and committing to that result.* That kind of decision requires you to be **unquenchable***, *a refusal to be talked out of your dream by refusing to be satisfied, subdued or to settle for less.*

When you make a no-matter-what decision, when situations arise, you decide how you're going to respond based on your desired outcome, not based on your feelings or emotions. As a result, you set yourself up to create the results you want.

3 **DEVELOP UNWAVERING FAITH.** "Faith assures us of things we expect and convinces us of the existence of things we cannot see." Hebrews 11:1, *God's Word Translation*. It is the well-grounded confidence and persuasion that what we hope for will actually happen. You have to have faith in your dream and your ability to bring it to fruition.

If you were to look up the definitions of the words dreamer and visionary, you would notice that it's not always seen as a positive thing to be a dreamer. According to *Merrian-Webster.com*, a dreamer is a person who is unpractical and idealistic, someone whose ideas or projects are considered audacious or highly speculative, a visionary. *Dictionary.com* defines visionary as one who tends to envision things in perfect but unrealistic form, an idealist, one who is given to impractical or speculative ideas, a dreamer.

Because others cannot always see the vision, they may dismiss it as unrealistic or impractical and may even classify you a **delusional dreamer***, *someone with false or unrealistic beliefs and expectations about what it will take to make their dreams a reality*. That's why faith is so important and such an integral part of every aspect of this journey. Because when no one else can see it and when others make you feel like you're crazy, it's your faith, your well-grounded confidence, that reminds you that it is possible and that encourages you to keep moving forward.

There is a thin line though between faith and delusion. Both are beliefs; however, faith is *based on good evidence and reason,* whereas a delusion *is a mistaken or misleading opinion, idea, or belief.* Under-stand the difference between the two and make sure that while you have faith, you are not a delusional dreamer.

With all that being said, *what do you want? What do you really want? Who do you want to be? What do you want to do? What do you want to create? What do you want to have in terms of possessions? What impact do you want to have in the lives of others?*

This is not the editing phase. This is an opportunity to dream about creating things the way you want them to be instead of accepting things the way they are. This is a time to really ask and answer for yourself, *what do you dare to dream?*

NOW WHAT

TAKE THE BUCKET LIST CHALLENGE.
Download the Dare to Dream Companion Guide for a simple step-by-step Bucket List How to and for information about the challenge.

ANCHORS & ACCELERATORS.
Make a list of the top five people you seek counsel and advice from. Identify who are the anchors and accelerators.

WHAT DO YOU DARE TO DREAM? #shareyours.
Record and upload a short video sharing what you dare to dream at **idaretodreamproject.com**.

Download the **DARE TO DREAM COMPANION GUIDE**

idaretodreamproject.com/d2dguide

HOW TO NOT BE A DELUSIONAL DREAMER

> **delusional dreamer**
> someone who has false or unrealistic beliefs and expectations about what it will take to make their dreams a reality

1. **DON'T KEEP YOUR DREAM IN YOUR HEAD.** Write it out. Talk it out. Then share it with others.

2. **DON'T ASSUME.** Seek out good counsel and know what it will take to make your dreams a reality based on where you currently are.

3. **DON'T MAKE EXCUSES AND DON'T PROCRASTINATE.** Take responsibility and make decisions. Start right where you are. You may not be able to do things to the scale you want yet, but you can still take action now.

4. **DON'T BE FAITHFUL TO YOUR FEARS.** You cannot fully commit to pursuing your dreams as long as you're faithful to fear, so break up with fear and refuse to allow it to be a hindrance or excuse.

5. **DON'T EXPECT TO BE AN OVERNIGHT SUCCESS.** This journey is a process and it takes as long as it takes and as long as you take.

6. **DON'T BE CHEAP.** People will come along and help you, but this is your dream and *you* have to be willing to make the necessary investments of time, money, and resources.

7. **DON'T THINK THAT FAITH AND SELF-CONFIDENCE IS ENOUGH.** "Faith without action is dead." James 2:17, *KJV*. Faith and self-confidence are important, but they are nothing without action.

8. **DON'T PUT YOUR LIFE AND RELATIONSHIPS ON HOLD UNTIL YOUR DREAM IS A REALITY.** Chances are, it will take longer than you think to get to where you want to be. So live your life as you pursue and make time for the people and things that are important to you.

9. **DON'T THINK THAT YOUR DREAM HAS TO BE BIG TO BE SPECIAL.** The worth of your dream is not determined by the size of your dream. The goal is for you to be true to the dreams of your heart, whether it's big or small.

10. **DON'T PURSUE IF YOU REALIZE THAT THE DREAM IS NO LONGER A FIT.** It's ok to change your mind if what you're pursuing no longer lines up with what you want and who you want to be. Just make sure you're not changing your mind because of fear, doubt, or insecurity.

WHAT IF IT WASN'T ABOUT BEING RIGHT? **WHAT IF YOU JUST GOT EXCITED BY QUESTIONS** LIKE WHAT DO YOU WANT, WHO DO YOU WANT TO BE, OR WHAT DO YOU DARE TO DREAM? **WHAT IF FINDING THE ANSWERS WAS AN ADVENTURE?**

IN SEARCH OF A DREAM
FOLLOW THE TRAILS

It starts with a dream
A goal, something bigger than you, that excites and challenges you
It starts with a dream
One that pushes and stretches you to live outside of your comfort zone
It starts with a dream
One that paints a new picture of what's possible and what life can be like
It starts with a dream
A simple idea, which connects with the purpose that lies inside of you and sparks and grows into an unquenchable passion that leaves you with no other choice, but to say yes
It Starts with a Dream, Valerie Jeannis, 2015

It all starts with a dream, but what do you do if you're not sure what your dream is?

For starters, relax. It's ok not to know. *But what if…? How? Who? What? When? Where? Why?*

So much pressure is put on having all the answers that we miss the most exciting aspect of questions – the discovery. Yes, a question is meant to elicit an answer, but it's also a seeking and the beginning of a discussion or journey.

What if it wasn't about being right? What if you started recognizing the potential that could be found in the quest that a question can lead you on? What if you just got excited by questions like, what do you want, who do you want to be, or what do you dare to dream? What if finding the answers was an adventure?

If you feel like you have a lot of options, then it becomes like a multiple-choice question or a game of elimination – which one isn't it? If you don't know what your options are, then it's more of a scavenger hunt where you're using what you do know to help you find and collect more clues. And as you collect the clues, like pieces in a puzzle, you'll start to see how everything fits together.

Regardless where you are, explore. Pay attention to the clues. Allow the process to take however long it takes, and most importantly, have fun. To kick-start the journey of finding your dream, follow the trails.

FOLLOW YOUR PASSION

We all have things we're passionate about, that we tend to go back to, that consumes our conversations, thoughts, and even the things we gravitate toward. As you pursue those passions, you'll start to see how one thing will often lead to something else you never really anticipated, which can eventually lead you to your dream and purpose.

Since I was eighteen years old, I've been passionate about empowering women and challenging them to never settle. At the time, I was in a very difficult relationship that I thought I would never get out of.

Because I didn't want to see other young girls go through the same things or make the same mistakes I made, I started a mentorship group with 13-15 year olds. That group lead to me pursuing both an undergraduate and master's degree in social work. Later, I decided that I wanted to start a residential non-for-profit organization (NPO) to help women aging out of foster care.

During graduate school, I reached out to one of my professors, Professor Brown-Manning, who took the time to really listen. After I shared the vision of what I wanted the organization to look like, she asked me one simple question that put things in perspective for me – *Do you really want to start a NPO or are you trying to force your vision for something else into a NPO model?*

That conversation helped me realize I actually did *not* want to start a NPO, it was just the only way I knew. **Often times we end up going down a particular path, not because we necessarily want to, but because we aren't aware of the different options that are available to us.** That's why it's important to do research, to speak to others and to learn about other people's journey. As you do, you will start to see just how many possibilities are available to you. Because stories are so powerful, the *I Dare to Dream Project* includes an interview series where those who dared to dream and pursue openly share their journeys and lessons learned along the way.

After realizing that I didn't want to start a NPO, I started searching for alternatives and discovered I could start a business where I empower people as an author, speaker, coach and trainer, which is what I do today. All of this started with my passion to empower women and a decision to follow that passion, even though I didn't know where it would lead.

What are you passionate about and what steps can you take today to start exploring those passions? Who can you reach out to for guidance and advice?

FOLLOW YOUR PAIN

If you ever looked into the origins of organizations such as To Write Love on Her Arms (TWLOHA.org), Mothers Against Drunk Driving, and the Breast Cancer Walk, to name a few, you would discover that they all started because of a pain or calamity that the founder(s) or someone close to them experienced. While there are certain things we will never fully understand when it comes to tragedy, **sometimes the hardest moments in our lives can reveal our life's call and purpose.**

There are defining moments after a tragedy when a decision must be made about what impact will this event have in your life. *Will it be a catalyst for positive change in your life and/or the life of others? Or will you allow it to rob you of your joy and sense of purpose and keep you anchored to a moment in time?* As difficult as it can be and as deep as the pain may run, **you can find purpose in pain.**

Think back to some of your most challenging moments. *What did those experiences teach you? Where you able to use what you've been through to help someone else? What kind of changes did you notice needed to be made, either for you personally or in your community? Did you want to be a part of helping make those changes?*

As you answer some of these questions, you will hopefully start to see that good can come from bad and that dreams can be conceived in the midst of pain.

FOLLOW ENCOURAGEMENT

Sometimes people will see greatness and potential in you before you see it in yourself. The following is a snippet from an email I received from someone I met briefly years ago when I was still full of so many blanks and question marks.

> Valerie,
> I hope you find a way to inspire other women your age to never be afraid to stand tall and to be proud of who they are… Your gift is connection, showing others what can be done when you hold onto your desire with determination. You dress the part of confidence; you also walk it and talk it. Share that passion with others who have fallen short of their dreams.
>
> Maybe teach them through stories and examples, how self-creation and growth is possible, even from the lowest of low places. Maybe your book could be about women who have found their way back and want to share their strengths and feelings of faith and hope.
>
> If you could inspire one woman who was down and trapped in her life to stand up and take on life with all the courage and determination you have found throughout the country or even the world, what a wonderful gift that would be. Valor-ie

Looking back at some of the points made so many years ago and what I am doing today, it's obvious this person saw certain pieces of the puzzle before I did. When I get caught up in the fog of doubt and insecurity, I am reminded of words such as those, often spoken by strangers whose paths I crossed for a moment in time, but who saw things in me that I didn't see in myself yet.

You cannot live on the words of people, but sometimes those words and the faith that they express in you, can serve as a lifeline until you are able to stand on your own faith and assurance of who you are and what's possible for your life. *What potential have people seen in you?*

If it's hard for you to see your gifts and talents or even if you think you already know what they are, interview people from different aspects of your life. Ask them what they see as your gifts, talents, and personal strengths. If you go to the website, you will be able to download the *Dare to Dream Companion Guide*, which also includes an interview form you can use.

Life is always giving us clues. Be on the lookout for them and pay attention. Even if the clues are not direct paths to your dream, remain open because they can bring you one step closer. You may find that the answers that you're looking for are closer than you think. You might even already know what they are and it's more a matter of giving yourself permission to go for it.

NOW WHAT

LEARN THE STORIES OF OTHERS.
Reach out to at least three people who you admire or who inspire you and ask them about how they found their dreams/ purpose. Be curious about their journey. There are some suggested questions included in the companion guide.

INTERVIEW PEOPLE FROM DIFFERENT ASPECTS OF YOUR LIFE.
You will find the interview form in the Companion Guide.

GET FEEDBACK.
Share your dream with an advisor or mentor and ask them for feedback.

WHAT DO YOU DARE TO DREAM? #shareyours.
Record and upload a short video sharing what you dare to dream at **idaretodreamproject.com**.

Download the **DARE TO DREAM COMPANION GUIDE**

idaretodreamproject.com/d2dguide

HOW TO FIND YOUR DREAM

> **dream**
> to imagine that you can be, do, have, or create something that exists first in your heart and mind only

1. **FOLLOW YOUR ACCOMPLISHMENTS.** What have you done that has given you the greatest sense of pride?

2. **FOLLOW YOUR COMPASSION.** Who do you want to help or make life better for?

3. **FOLLOW YOUR CONVERSATIONS.** What are you constantly talking about?

4. **FOLLOW YOUR CURIOSITY.** What are you curious about?

5. **FOLLOW YOUR DESIRES.** What do you want more of?

6. **FOLLOW YOUR ENTHUSIASM.** What excites and fuels you?

7. **FOLLOW YOUR FRUSTRATIONS.** What do you see or hear happening that really bothers you? What social problem would you change if you had the power?

8 **FOLLOW YOUR JOY.** What makes you happy? What seems to make time stand still for you?

9 **FOLLOW YOUR MONEY.** What do you spend your money on?

10 **FOLLOW YOUR TIME.** What do you spend your time doing? What do you watch on TV? Beyond the drama, what is it about the show(s) that speaks to you or keeps you tuning in?

LIKE A SPARK THAT IGNITES A FOREST FIRE, **AN IDEA**, WHICH CONNECTS WITH THE PURPOSE THAT LIES INSIDE OF YOU, **CAN GROW INTO AN UNQUENCHABLE DREAM** THAT LEAVES YOU WITH NO OTHER CHOICE BUT TO SAY YES.

SOMETHING OUTSIDE + SOMETHING INSIDE
CONCEPTION OF A DREAM

Isn't it amazing how one moment can change your life? How something that seems so common or that you do all the time can start something so extraordinary without you even realizing it?

For Jaylene Clark Owens, her moment came in the form of a Facebook status update where she wrote, *"It's time to stop dipping a toe in here/ Wading in a little bit there/ I need to jump back into this Sea World of poetry like I'm Shamu/ Heavy/ Too much gentrification going on in Harlem to get light/ Time to spit killer lines, with killer rhymes, of killer tales/ Cuz Harlem is looking more and more like the belly of a killer whale."*

Alfred Preisser, who taught Jaylene when she attended the Harlem School of the Arts College Prep theater program, saw the status update and asked her if she could create an entire show based on the killer whale/gentrification metaphor that would incorporate theater and spoken word for his play reading series at the Schomburg Center for Research in Black Culture. Jaylene, who always wanted to create a show that blended her two loves, theater and poetry, jumped on the opportunity. What started out as a simple status update turned into an awarding-winning play with four young ladies that had sold out shows across the country.

$$I^2 + P^2 = D_2D$$

(INSPIRATION & IDEAS) + (PASSION & PURPOSE)
SOMETHING OUTSIDE + SOMETHING INSIDE

= THE DREAM YOU DARE TO DREAM

Like a spark that ignites a forest fire, an idea, which connects with the purpose that lies inside of you, can grow into an unquenchable dream that leaves you with no other choice but to say yes.

The **conception of a dream*** is *a process where something outside of you, an inspiration or idea, connects with something inside of you, your passion or purpose, and as a result of a continual yes, develops into a dream.*

In Jaylene's case, the request by her instructor to create a show based on her status update (*something outside of her*) connected with her passions for theater and poetry (*something inside of her*) and the play, "In the Belly of a Killer Whale" (*the dream*), was conceived. Without the influence of her professor, that status would have probably been just another good status update that eventually got filed away in the archives.

That's why it's important to interact with people and your environment and one of the main reasons why I love attending seminars. To be in a space with like-minded people from all over the world gathering with an open mind and open heart, people who are there to give as much as they are to receive, is beyond words. In fact, two of the major personal shifts in my life occurred while at seminars.

THE PLANTING OF A SEED

When I wrote that bucket list at Breakthrough to Success, I never thought that taking the time to do so would have changed my life, but it did. After I received that trip to Disney World, I started looking at my list to see what else did I really want to go after. Some of the other things on my list included:

- To become an entrepreneur
- To empower women and youth
- To travel to all 50 states by December 30, 2014
- To interview entrepreneurs and CEOs

I didn't know how any of those things were going to happen and it didn't matter because I was reassured that the how would come. Sure enough, it did. Seven months later in March 2010, while taking notes at Experts' Academy, a seminar by Brendon Burchard, this idea came to me, "*Why don't you travel to all 50 states interviewing women from all walks of life in order to empower young women and youth?*" A concept from Experts Academy and the bucket list from Breakthrough to Success (*something outside of me*) connected with my passion to empower women and youth and my desire to travel (*something inside of me*), and the idea for *I Dare to Dream Project* (*the dream*) was conceived.

A PASSING IDEA OR A DREAM WORTH PURSUING

All dreams start out as ideas, but not all ideas turn into dreams worth pursuing. So *how do you know if your idea is just a passing idea or a dream worth pursuing?*

1. **TIME.** When you have a dream worth pursuing, over time your commitment to that dream will become stronger, whereas your commitment to a passing idea will fade.

2. **AN INNER KNOWING.** Sometimes you just know. You'll have thoughts like, "*It just doesn't feel right*" or "*I just know that this is it*". **Just because you're not always able to explain the feeling does not discredit its validity.** It may not be enough for some people, but it should be for you, especially as you learn to trust yourself.

3. **THE P TEST***, *a test of passion and purpose*. When it's a dream worth pursuing, it's consuming. It becomes a part of you. It engages and captures your imagination. It dictates your choices. In short, it's a passion. *See Companion Guide for test.*

From the very beginning this is a walk of faith where you will be making decisions based on what you believe, more so than on what you see or know for a fact. Sometimes it will be very obvious whether or not you should pursue a particular idea, other times not so much. Don't let that stop you from moving forward.

There are so many things that can impact the course of your life. Among those things is a dream, which starts out as an idea that you dare to pursue.

	A PASSING IDEA	A DREAM WORTH PURSUING
PASSION	Phases out over time; Forgettable	Continues to grow; Constantly on your mind; Consuming
PURPOSE	May be related or in the same field, but it is not an exact match	Is connected to your purpose
ENTHUSIASM	Was never really there; May have just gotten excited about what was connected to the idea instead of the idea itself	Increases over time (though there may be dips at times, which is normal)
CREATIVITY	Engages and captures your imagination, but with no commitment	Engages and captures your imagination, with the commitment to follow through
COMMITMENT	Unwilling to make great sacrifices or any that would disrupt norm or comfort	Willing to make sacrifices; Becomes a pressing priority that takes precedence over almost everything
CHALLENGES	May cause you to walk away or for your commitment to waiver	Still say yes in spite of
INSTINCT	Something inside of you just says no or not now	Personal conviction; Something inside of you just says yes
TIME	Little to no growth	Shows growth over time; An increase in passion, excitement and commitment

WHEN YOU BREAK UP WITH FEAR, YOU ARE CHOOSING TO **MAKE YOUR DREAM MORE IMPORTANT** THAN WHAT YOU ARE AFRAID OF.

MONSTERS UNDER MY BED
FEAR

Have you ever seen a child who is afraid to sleep at night because they believe they have monsters under their bed? Even though you know there really are no monsters, you cannot deny their fear. Often they are imagining things that aren't there or misinterpreting things that are.

As illogical as their fears can be, they originated from somewhere and if they are not properly dealt with, they can become a real hindrance.

When it comes to the fears that keep us from going after our dreams, they can be like monsters under the bed. We convince ourselves that there's something out there to be afraid of and we allow those thoughts to influence and even dictate our choices.

Fear causes us to give up prematurely or to walk away without even trying. It suffocates our dreams, robs us of hope, and cripples our progress. It's the main culprit behind the three major factors that cause people to consider aborting their dreams:

1. **THE FEAR FACTOR**, which usually stems from a negative what-if statement. *What if I fail? What if it doesn't work? What if they laugh at me?*

2. **THE PEOPLE FACTOR**, which involves dealing with other people's opinions and judgments about you and your dream.

3   **THE CONFIDENCE FACTOR**, which involves your opinion and judgments about yourself, your dream and your ability to successfully pursue.

Really it's all fear, which can be divided in two categories – internal dialogue, *the conversations in our head*, and external pressures and influences involving *people and circumstances*.

VOICES IN OUR HEADS

Part of what contributes to the internal dialogue that feeds our fears are the voices in our head. There are three main types of voices that will try to influence the choices you make.

1   **THE VOICE OF AUTHORITY.** As great as it is to have mentors we respect, often times we can value their opinion above our own because of their accomplishments or positions. The danger is taking their advice, even when you don't fully agree or when something inside of you is telling you to pursue a different route.

2   **THE VOICE OF LOVED ONES.** Though they may have good intentions, the feedback of friends and loved ones can lead to doubt and stress, instead of faith and encouragement. They may discourage you from pursuing your dream, try to encourage you down a path *they* feel is best for you, or try to limit you or make you feel guilty for wanting what you want.

3. **THE VOICE OF DOUBT.** The voice of doubt is the voice of fear. It usually speaks from bad past experiences or your own limited view or opinion of yourself and your abilities. It will always try to talk you out of taking leaps of faith and into staying where you are, even if it's painful.

While there are negative voices in our heads, there is also your inner voice, a still small voice reminding you you can do this. Your inner voice leads, guides, teaches, prompts, inspires and urges you by showing you what to do, when to do it and who to partner with. It's the part of you that seems to know the answers to the question even if you cannot always logically explain why that's the answer. Some think it's the universe speaking to them; I believe it's the Creator of the universe. Unlike the other voices, your inner voice speaks from a place of faith and possibility.

Even when you have faith and believe, every now and then, there can be these overwhelming bouts of fear that we allow to make us fall short of following through. We all have moments when we're afraid; however, when fear starts dictating the choices you make and keeping you from the things you want, then it's time to **break up with fear*,** *to make a choice and a declaration to no longer allow fear to hinder, cripple or stop you from pursuing your dreams or going after anything you want.*

Breaking up with fear is about changing your relationship with fear. It doesn't mean that fear will no longer show up or try to influence you. It does means that when it does, and it will, you can remind it and yourself of the choice you made to move forward in spite of. When you break up with fear, you are choosing to make your dream more important than what you're afraid of.

Whether it's the internal dialogue or the external influences and pressures, the ultimate question when it comes to your dream is, *which voice will you listen to – the voice of fear or the voice of faith and possibilities?*

I DARE TO DREAM PROJECT

idaretodreamproject.com/dearfear

DEAR

IT'S OVER!

FEAR

HOW TO BREAK UP WITH FEAR

> **breaking up with fear**
> a choice and a declaration to no longer allow fear to hinder, cripple, or stop you from pursuing your dreams or going after anything that you want

1. **KNOW WHAT YOU WANT OR DON'T WANT.** There has to be something that you either want really bad or don't want bad enough that it overrides the fear.

2. **CALL FEAR OUT.** Identify all of the fears that are coming up for you when you think about your dream.

3. **CHECK THE SOURCE.** Where did those fears come from? They may not even be your fears and may have been passed down from others.

4. **CHALLENGE THE FEARS WITH TRUTH.** Fear is a liar. It will misconstrue or try to make you forget the truth in an attempt to cause you to quit or play small. Think back to fears that you've overcome. It helps to be reminded that fear can be conquered.

5. **PUT YOUR FEARS TO THE TEST.** Do the thing that you're afraid of. Most fears are invalid and threatening shadows of unlikely possibilities.

6 **HAVE A PLAN AND GET SUPPORT.** Some fears require a bit of strategy. Reach out for support and create a plan of attack to overcome your fears. You don't have to do it alone.

7 **BE PATIENT WITH YOURSELF.** There may be times that you'll give in to the fear. Learn from those moments and then keep moving forward.

8 **COUNT THE COST. FOCUS ON THE PRIZE.** Remember what fear has or can cost you. Remember what you're fighting for and what you stand to gain every time you stand up to fear. Allow those things to motivate you.

9 **CELEBRATE THE WINS.** Every time you take a step forward in spite of your fears, write it down and celebrate yourself, even if it's just taking a moment to smile and literally give yourself a pat on the back.

10 **TELL FEAR IT'S OVER.** Write a breakup letter to fear. Write about how fear has influenced, changed, or hindered you and your choices. Then write down what will now be possible because you're no longer allowing fear to control you. Submit your letter at **idaretodreamproject.com/dearfear**.

YOU CANNOT ALLOW SOMEONE ELSE'S OPINION TO DETERMINE WHAT YOU CAN OR CANNOT DO OR WHAT YOU WILL OR WILL NOT DO. AT SOME POINT, YOU HAVE TO **LEARN TO TRUST YOURSELF**...

THE WEIGHT OF AN OPINION
SOMEONE ELSE SAID SO

I used to babysit my 2-year-old godson, who was incredibly hyperactive. One moment he would be sitting next to me, the next he would be literally half way up a cabinet. Because of that, I was always afraid that he would hurt himself. Every time I didn't see him for a few seconds or he started getting up, I would scream out his name in a panic and whenever he asked for or reached for anything, my answer would usually be no. I loved him and wanted him to be happy, but my priority was keeping him safe. It would have been easy for him to think I was being mean, but really I was scared and trying to shield him from danger the best way I knew.

It's one thing when those in your life set out to hurt you. It's another thing when they hurt you while attempting to protect you. Depending on their personal experiences and perspective, there will be people, who you love and who love you, who will tell you no or try to discourage you when you share your dreams with them. Though their hearts are in the right place, parents tend to be guilty of this. In a misguided attempt to keep you safe, they may use their position, influence, or relation-ship to force their dreams for you on you, often leaving you feeling powerless to go after what *you* really want. They may even go so far as to threaten to withdraw their financial support knowing that they are your sole or primary means of financial support.

LEARNING TO TRUST YOURSELF

Whether or not it's coming from a place of love, you cannot allow someone else's opinion to determine what you can or cannot do (*your beliefs*) or what you will or will not do (*your actions*). At some point, **you have to learn to trust yourself and follow your heart**, which may be the hardest thing you learn to do.

I once ran into a beautiful actress in the fruit section of the supermarket. What started out as a simple hello turned into a conversation about life and choices. She shared how on the day of her wedding, she stood outside the church doors holding her father's arm, and when the music started playing and her father was ready to take a step forward, she held him in place shaking her head no.

Her dad looked at her and told her, "*Listen, I paid a lot of money and there are a lot of people sitting in there waiting for you. Come on.*" Even though she knew it was a mistake, even though she changed her mind and no longer wanted to marry this man, even though everything inside of her was screaming for her to run, she walked down the aisle anyway and said, "*I do.*"

When I asked her why, she responded, "*If my dad would have said, 'Baby, don't worry about it. If you don't want to do this, you don't have to. You go and I'll take care of everything else,' I would never have done it. But he didn't and I didn't know how to say no.*" Unfortunately, her doubts proved to be right. After being cheated on for years, she finally found the strength to do what she wanted to do that day at the church – walk away.

As I walked home that night, I couldn't help but wonder, *how many times do we do things in spite of ourselves? How many times do we feel uneasiness about people and directions we are getting ready to take, but we ignore it? How many times do we feel lead down a certain path or we change our minds about continuing down the path that we're currently on, but we choose to ignore our inner voice and to listen to people instead? How many times do we have an idea or a dream that we want to pursue, but we allow someone else to talk us of it? Or to talk us into going after what they want us to pursue? How many times have you done it?*

We are divinely guided people and continuously given insight regarding situations and questions we have. We just have to become better listeners and more intentional about tuning in to God and our internal guidance system.

One way to start recognizing your inner voice is by looking for patterns. Think back to different situations in the past when you had questions about a choice you had to make and you just knew what the right answer for you was. Even if you couldn't explain how you knew that was the right choice, you just knew. Regardless whether or not you listened, that was your inner voice. Think of other moments in your life when you had this similar sense of knowing. As you start to notice the patterns, it will become easier to distinguish your inner voice and to get answers to your questions. What you choose to do with that information is your choice.

THE POWER OF CHOICE

There was a time when you had to live according to the choices of others. You had to do what you were told, go where you were told, sleep when you were told, and eat what you were told. You are no longer a child and you can now exercise the **power of choice***, *the power to decide for yourself what you want in any given situation.*

But let's be honest, there are times when you want someone else to make the hard decisions for you. You want them to tell you whether or not you should go after your dream or down a certain path. That way, if things don't work out, you can just pass the blame.

Having someone else make the hard choices can feel easier. However, even when you try to blame someone else for *your* choice when you don't like the outcome, *you're* the one who has to live with the consequences. **The "just tell me what to do" attitude and mindset will only make you a functional dependent and will most likely delay you from living your dream, if you ever go after it at all.** You have to make decisions for yourself. Even when your decision is unpopular or one that causes others to misunderstand or misjudge you, you must exercise the power of choice.

LEARNING TO CARE LESS

There is a story told about a young boy who entered a barbershop where the barber whispered to his customer, "This is the dumbest kid in the world. Watch while I prove it to you." The barber placed a dollar bill in one hand and two quarters in the other, then called the boy over and asked, "Which do you want, son?" The boy took the quarters and left.

The barber turned to his customer and said, "What did I tell you? That kid never learns!"

Later, when the customer left, he saw the same young boy coming out of the ice cream store and asked him, "Why did you take the quarters instead of the dollar bill?" The boy licked his cone and replied, "Because the day I take the dollar, the game is over!"

It turns out the dumbest kid in the world might not be so dumb after all. Somewhere along the way he learned a lesson that we all need to learn – *who cares what people think about you?* He was willing to look stupid and to accept people talking negatively about him in order to get what he wanted. *Are you willing to do the same?*

One of the reasons that we have a hard time pursuing what we want when we know others want something else for us is because, whether we admit it or not, we want the approval of certain people in our lives. While that's understandable, you have to free yourself from the need for the validation of others. You have to learn to care less.

It really is that simple. Simple, but not easy. If you want to freely pursue your dreams and to execute the different ideas that will help you actually birth those dreams, you have to make up your mind to care less, even when the truth is you actually do care. People's opinions and validation cannot be more important to you than it is for you to actually be true to yourself and your dreams. Besides, it takes too much energy to constantly be concerned about how people will receive and respond to what you are doing. So care less. It may be a mildly aggressive statement, but it's also a very liberating one.

Seriously, *does everyone have to agree with you? Does everyone have to think your idea is great? Does everyone have to be excited about what you're pursuing? Isn't it enough that you're excited? And if it isn't, shouldn't it be?*

FIGHT FOR IT

The pursuit of your dreams is not a democracy dependent on majority approval. People have the right to their opinions, just like you have the right to politely disagree and to move forward anyway. Even if it's an unpopular choice, **find a way to stand for your dreams. If you don't, the consequences, regret and loss will be yours first, then it will be for every single person you were meant to touch and who needed what you had to offer.**

Part of daring to dream is a willingness to fight for you dream. It is *not* about fighting people, so don't waste your time trying to convince anyone of the validity of your dream. Instead, invest your energy in nurturing, protecting, and developing the dream that you are carrying.

And here's a little secret: When you stick to your decision and work to make your dreams a reality, many of your naysayers will be the very same ones who show up and tell you how great you are and how they knew you were going to make it the whole time. They will even offer their support. As tempting as it will be to roll your eyes or to remind them of what they really thought, don't get bitter. Say thank you because their doubt and negativity may have been the very motivation you needed to make the choices that were crucial to your success.

NOW WHAT

FOOD FOR THOUGHT.
Where are you allowing the opinions of other to keep you from going after what you want?

Looking forward to what you want and where you want to be, what new choices can you start to make now?

WRITE A BREAKUP LETTER TO FEAR.
Follow the steps of how to break up with fear. Then, write a breakup letter to fear and submit it at **idaretodreamproject.com/DearFear**

WHAT DO YOU DARE TO DREAM? #shareyours.
Record and upload a short video sharing what you dare to dream at **idaretodreamproject.com**.

YOU **CAN** DO THIS.
YOU **CAN** PURSUE YOUR
DREAMS. YOUR DREAMS
CAN BECOME A REALITY.

DISTORTED VIEW
I CAN'T DO THIS

On February 26, 2013, the day before my 28th birthday, I sat in a meeting and listened as someone, whom I respected and looked up to, questioned everything I was working toward, even my motives. Thinking back, I can't even remember exactly what was said. I just recall being taken aback to the point of tears.

After trying desperately to regain my composure, I was finally able to keep it together long enough, to say thank you for the meeting and leave. While I'm sure it wasn't their intention, I felt like I was hit… hard… and bleeding. I walked home that night in tears questioning everything. I started doubting myself, my dream, my ability to get the necessary support and wondering if anyone would even care about my project, let alone want to participate.

All I wanted to do was get under the covers, cry myself to sleep, and not wake up until really, really late the next day. Fortunately, that wasn't an option. I had a speaking engagement at an alternative high school downtown Brooklyn.

Needless to say, I wasn't in the best frame of mind nor was I feeling entirely confident. It didn't help that I overslept and woke up with puffy eyes, that it was raining, and that I arrived to the school late. Not exactly the best start for a happy birthday.

BEYOND A SHADOW OF A DOUBT

Have you ever had one of those moments when you knew beyond a shadow of a doubt that you were doing exactly what you were meant to do? I've heard other people talk about it, but I've never experienced it until that day. As I stood in front of a room full of students, who were literally staring me down, I was what only I could be – myself. I gave them all of me. And while I was speaking, I watched as the students actually leaned in to listen to what I was saying. It was at that moment that I was overcome with this knowing, this absolute conviction that this is exactly what I'm supposed to be doing with my life. **It didn't matter that others didn't see it yet. It didn't matter that I wasn't the best yet.** It didn't even matter that I didn't know how yet. I knew I was where I was supposed to be and doing what I was supposed to be doing and that was more than enough.

If you look at a caterpillar, there's nothing about it that would suggest that inside of this slithering creature there are wings. So ordinary looking, yet destined to be beautiful, destined to fly. Whether you believe it yet or not, there is more to you than what meets the eyes. You may look at yourself and see ordinary, average, or even insignificant, but like the caterpillar, you are extra-ordinary.

You have to go through a process first in order to bring what's inside outside, but trust and believe that everything you need to become who you're meant to be, you already possess. It's up to you to start owning that fact.

I CAN'T DO THIS

We often tell ourselves that we can't do something, not because we really doubt our ability to do it, but because we're afraid to try and fail. We convince ourselves that we won't be able to handle failure.

To dare to dream is to risk failure. There's no way around that. There will be times you go after something and you will miss the mark. In those moments you can choose to give up and think self-defeating thoughts such as, *"I knew I couldn't do this. Things never work out for me. They were right,"* or you can choose to be an **extraordinary failure***, *someone who stepped out and attempted something that they did not get, but something even greater than they imagined happened because they did not give up.*

To be an extraordinary failure is an honor that very few people receive because not everyone is willing to put themselves out there, fail, and still keep moving forward until they reach their goals or something better. **That's the extraordinary part, to be willing to try and try again with the sting of failure still fresh in your mind and the voice of doubt loud in your ears.**

As painful as it was, I am grateful the *I Dare to Dream Project* didn't occur when and how I originally planned because so many great things, including this book, wouldn't have happened. I'm not telling you to actually set yourself up to fail. I *am* saying that you don't have to be afraid of failing because if it does happen, it can position you for something greater than you originally planned.

YOU GOT THIS

It would be great if we had faith in ourselves all the time, but we don't. There are moments when we panic and think all kinds of crazy negative things. **However, when doubts come and you have trouble seeing it for yourself, lean on those who will remind you that you got this, because you do.** You've made it this far. You may not always feel like you're making progress, but you are. Give yourself some credit. Acknowledge and celebrate yourself for the things you *have* accomplished.

As you pursue your dreams you will set out to discover and accomplish one thing, and along the way you will do so much more than you ever anticipated. You will conquer giants, challenge old, invalid beliefs, and discover new worlds both within and around you. You will meet new people, form your own beliefs about what's true for you, and in the end, regardless what happens, you will discover that you lived. Not just existed, but really lived. You *can* do this. You can pursue your dreams. And your dreams can become a reality. Trust. Trust the process. Trust yourself. Just trust.

NOW WHAT

REMIND YOURSELF YOU CAN.
Create a list of at least 10 reasons why you know that you can do make your dreams a reality.

REMIND YOURSELF YOU MUST.
Create a list of at least 5 reasons why you must make your dreams a reality.

ARE YOU AN EXTRAORDINARY FAILURE?
Share your story.
idaretodreamproject.com/submissions.

WRITE A BREAKUP LETTER TO FEAR.
Follow the steps of how to break up with fear. Then, write a breakup letter to fear and submit it at **idaretodreamproject.com/dearfear**

WHAT DO YOU DARE TO DREAM? #shareyours.
Record and upload a short video sharing what you dare to dream at **idaretodreamproject.com**.

How to be an Extraordinary Failure

> **extraordinary failure**
> someone who stepped out and attempted something they did not get, but something even greater than they imagined happened because they did not give up.

1. Attempt something great.
2. Do your absolute best so that there are no regrets.
3. Miss the mark you set out to hit (not on purpose, of course).
4. Learn and grow and refuse to give up.
5. Ignore the naysayers.
6. Recognize the unique opportunity that your "failure" has now presented you with.
7. Dare to dream a new dream or go after the same dream again.
8. Succeed, even if it looks different than you originally thought.
9. Have fun and enjoy the journey.
10. Share your story, inspire and support others.

NEVER ENOUGH
A MINDSET ISSUE

Three days before she died of cancer, Sarah called her friend Jodie and begged Jodie to promise she would pursue her dream of traveling around the world. Jodie felt torn. Even though it was her dream to travel and she wanted to promise her friend she would do it, she didn't want to lie. She tried explaining she didn't have the money, but Sarah refused to take no for an answer.

"Promise," she said.

So Jodie promised.

A few months later, Jodie, who originally said no to her dreams because of her lack of finances, packed her bags and traveled the world for a year.

As I sat next to her and listened to her share her story, she turned to me and asked, *"Why does it have to take something like that to make us go after our dreams?"* At first I didn't know what to say. In the end though, **it really comes down to one thing, a decision. A conscious and deliberate no matter what decision that would not allow excuses or circumstances to be a hindrance**. A decision to trust that somehow, everything that was needed will manifest and be provided.

We are really good at coming up with excuses about why we cannot pursue our dreams. At the top of our list is usually lack of time, lack of money and lack of resources. Sorry to burst your bubble, actually, I'm not sorry. The fact is it's rarely a resource issue. It's a mindset and decision issue. If you're currently in a tight place financially, you may beg to differ. However, challenges cannot stop you; it's how you view those challenges that get in your way.

Pursuing your dreams is a walk of faith where provision follows the decision. If you're waiting for money, people, time, or whatever else you convince yourself you need in order to start, then you may be waiting for something that might not come until after you start. You have to be so invested in making your dreams a reality that even with the odds against you, you're still willing to say yes and take action. Provision will follow that kind of passion and commitment, and so will the people you need.

Instead of complaining about what you don't have or allowing excuses for not taking action, start asking the right questions. That can be the difference between moving forward and staying stuck. When you make declarations such as, "I never have enough money," your situation generally won't change. Instead, if you start asking questions like, *"How can I get the money that I need?"* then you open yourself up to inspiration.

You cannot afford to wait for everything to line up to go after what you want. Right where you are, you have to make up your mind to pursue, knowing or simply trusting that you'll have everything you need when you need it. You may not be able to do what you want to the scale you want right away, but you can still take daily steps, big or small, toward your dreams.

DON'T MISS IT

When I needed it most, provision came. Not in the form of money, like I expected and really, really wanted, but in the form of ideas, such as the idea for this book. **We often miss provisions when they come, because they don't show up the way we expect.** One of the common ways provision shows up is in the form of ideas.

Since we get ideas all the time, more often than not, when we get them, we dismiss them. We see them like pennies on the street, common and too small to be worth the effort. What we forget is that like pennies, ideas are the foundations that everything we see around us are built upon. One idea, one small, seemingly insignificant idea, can be the difference between the life you're living and the life you could only imagine living. It can be the difference between existence and significance. It can be the difference between poverty and wealth. An idea that you choose to pursue can change the course of your life, touch someone else's life, impact a generation and perhaps even change the world.

For me it started with an idea – *What if I traveled to all fifty states interviewing successful women?* It would have been easy to dismiss it, but because I didn't, that simple idea evolved and shifted the course of my life.

IT'S ALL FEAR

Most of the times we dismiss our ideas because of fear - fear of judgment, fear of rejection, fear of commitment, fear of lack, fear of inadequacy, fear of failure, fear of success. When it comes down to it, it's all fear. Even though faith is right there saying, *"You can do it. It's going to be such an adventure,"* too often, we give in to our fears. We allow fear to comfort us with lies such as; *it's better this way; it wouldn't have worked out anyway; you don't have time; you have more important things to do;*

you have responsibilities; you really dodged a bullet.

Fear is a liar. *Can you just imagine if everyone gave into those kinds of thoughts?* Think about it. If everyone gave in to their fears, our world would look so different today. All the things you love, all the things that make life comfortable for you, all the little luxuries, all the medical advances, none of it would exist if people didn't choose to say yes to their ideas and just go for it in spite of.

I DON'T KNOW AND NEITHER DO YOU

What can I say that will challenge you to give your ideas a chance? What can I say that will challenge you to not allow what you don't have to cause you to give up on what you want or on your ideas? I don't know. And in fact, that's the answer – I don't know and neither do you.

You don't know what will happen if you pursue. You don't know the difference it could make or the impact that it could have. You don't know where it will lead you or who it will lead you to. You don't know if it's the missing piece to the puzzle you're trying to figure out. You don't know and you will never know as long as you keep dismissing your ideas as insignificant or making excuses for why your dreams can't happen.

It's true that not all of our ideas are gold, and some really should not go any further than being a thought. But if you're honest with yourself and if you take the time to tune in to your inner voice, you will know the difference.

Provision follows a decision and often comes in the form of ideas. So list your ideas. Explore them. Decide if you want to pursue them. But do not simply dismiss them.

NOW WHAT

JOURNAL OF IDEAS.
What challenges and limitations are you currently facing when it comes to your dreams?

Come up with at least 10 ideas for how you can overcome each challenge. Have fun with it.

Purchase a pocket size journal that you keep with you to jot down your ideas. Don't judge your ideas or filter them. Just write down whatever comes to mind.

WRITE A BREAKUP LETTER TO FEAR. share yours.
Submit your letter online at **idaretodreamproject.com/DearFear**.

WHAT DO YOU DARE TO DREAM? #shareyours.
Record and upload a short video sharing what you dare to dream at **idaretodreamproject.com**.

SOMETIMES WE ABORT OUR DREAMS BY SAYING NO AND CHOOSING NOT TO PURSUE. OTHER TIMES, IT'S BY LIVING THE SMALLEST, SAFEST VERSION OF OUR DREAMS...

THE CONSEQUENCES
THE COST OF NO

I often think of the day when I saw my mother as I was walking down the street and immediately changed direction, hoping she didn't see me. Even as she called out my name over and over, I just kept on walking without looking back. We weren't fighting and I wasn't mad at her, I simply did not want to be around her or anyone else at that moment. I especially did not want to be in the apartment, which is where I was heading before changing my mind.

I didn't know what was wrong, but there I was walking down the streets in tears with no destination in mind. At least if something had happened what I was feeling would have made sense. I was writing, my speaking career was building momentum, things were good at home, and everything was as it always was – same apartment, same room, same me, same mundane routine, day in and day out. Turns out, that was the problem – it was all the same and I felt like I was suffocating. Once again I was in a place where the life I was living was not enough.

Somewhere along the way I settled for what was easier and comfortable. I didn't even realize that was what was causing my feelings of restlessness and frustration until I had a unique coaching session with Certified Dream Coach(tm), Caroll Michel Schwartz. She interviewed my inner voices to help identify what I really wanted and which doubts or fears were stopping me. It was a unique eye opening experience.

There are so many ways that we abort our dreams. Sometimes it's by saying no and choosing not to pursue. Other times it's by living the smallest, safest version of our dreams, which is what I was doing and I was starting to experience the consequences of that choice.

When you choose to walk away from your dream, not just a passing idea, but a dream that really connects with something inside of you, you do so at a risk. The most common aftermath you might experience are:

1 **THE WHAT-IF SYNDROME**, regret.

2 **RECKLESS BEHAVIOR**, activities you engage in to either help you feel or help you forget.

3 **A CYCLE OF QUITTING**, repeat behavior.

All of these can lead to a place of hopelessness where it starts to feel like nothing really matters. But there's hope.

THE WHAT-IF SYNDROME

One of the main risks of saying no to your dream is the **What-If Syndrome***, when *you are constantly taunted by the dream you gave up on and you fantasize about what could have been.* In one word, regret.

What leads us to making choices that we later regret or don't have peace about is when before making a decision we ask what-if followed by a negative statement. *What if I don't make it? What if I can't recover? What if I don't get the support that I need? What If I waste my time and miss out?* With those kind of what-ifs playing in our minds, it's no wonder we opt for the safe choice with minimal risk.

Even if you go on to do great things, if you haven't made peace with the choices of your past, they may come back to "haunt" you when you least expect. The negative what-ifs can lead to feelings of restlessness, and an intense desire for more than the life that you're living. It can also cause increase frustration and anger that you take out on the world or those closest to you, when in actuality you're really just mad at yourself or whomever you choose to blame for why *you* made the choice *you* made.

You can play out the different scenarios in your mind, but you'll never really know what could have happened if you made a different choice. One thing you can know for sure is that second chances are possible and that it's not too late. **You get to dream again.**

RECKLESS

In order to deal with the feelings of loss, frustration, and confusion that often come after an aborted dream, some check out and engage in reckless behavior, which results from two extremes:

1. **A FEELING OF NOTHINGNESS,** where you feel numb and as though nothing really matters, and you will do anything, good or bad, to simply feel again.

2. **AN OVERWHELMING AMOUNT OF FEELINGS,** where you are constantly thinking about what woulda, coulda, and shoulda been, so you engage in any activity, good or bad, that will help you forget or that you can lose yourself in, even if it's just for a moment.

Both extremes can lead to any of the following:

- Foolish Investments, often in materialistic things that may cause you to look better in people's eyes, but that don't support or encourage your growth or true feelings of self-worth,
- Poor choices, especially in relationships since part of you is seeking acceptance from others,
- Self-harm and destructive behavior including drug abuse, drinking, smoking, promiscuity, excessive overeating, etc,
- Separation from those who hold you accountable and/or who challenge you because they remind you of the dream or of an ideal that you no longer feel you can live up to,
- A new more accommodating circle of "friends" who "accept" you just the way you are and make it ok for you to be complacent since, among them, your average is seen as normal or even great,
- Becoming a workaholic in search of success and validation,

- Altruistic work driven by guilt and a need for penance.

In essence, you're engaging in all these activities to deal with how you're feeling without actually dealing with the real root problem. These are often a cry for help and a plea for someone to notice and care, even if that someone is you. Regardless of what you feel or what choices you've made, it's not too late. **You get to dream again.**

A CYCLE OF QUITTING

Once you walk away from or give up on something that means so much, you may find that it becomes easier to walk away from other important things or to just keep giving up.

You may notice that when you have a great idea, you start pursuing it, but then you give up. You get another idea that you're excited about and start pursuing, but you give up on that as well. Even when you want to do better, it seems to always end the same way, with you quitting and adding another incomplete to your list.

Repeat behavior can become automatic behavior, creating cycles. Your thoughts become poisoned by negativity and are then consumed by all your fears, doubts, anger and what you think others are saying. Your opinion of yourself also disintegrates and you start seeing yourself as a failure, a starter but never a finisher, an "incomplete", a quitter. Regardless of how many times you have tried in the past and it didn't work, it's not too late. **You get to dream again.**

NOW WHAT

FOOD FOR THOUGHT.
Have you walked away from a dream that you were really passionate about?

Do you want to go after it again?

WRITE A BREAKUP LETTER TO FEAR. share yours.
Submit your letter at
idaretodreamproject.com/DearFear.

WHAT DO YOU DARE TO DREAM? #shareyours.
Record and upload a short video sharing what you dare to dream at **idaretodreamproject.com**.

DARE TO DREAM AGAIN
A SECOND CHANCE

I let go of the shame of yesterday
I shake off the debris of regret
I release imprisoned hope
I lay hold of the promise of renewal

Potential caged is released
Ideas suppressed are released
Creations and suggestions
Topics and themes
Conferences and workshops
Relationships and friends

Endless possibilities I can now embrace
Because I learned to first let go
Let Go, Valerie Jeannis, 2015

"I'm *** Miserable."

    Personally I don't curse because I don't feel it's necessary. However, when that statement was made after I asked someone if they were happy, I almost felt like getting up and applauding.

    It was so honest that it was refreshing. The words jumped off the screen unapologetically and all I could type back in response was *"GREAT! Now what are you going to do about it?"*

If we're ever really honest with ourselves, we might be surprised by what shows up. You may find that you're frustrated, bored, and even miserable, all because of what could have been and a choice you made once about a time to abort your dream.

Whether you chose to walk away, pursue a smaller, safer version of your dream, or made choices that sabotaged your dream, it's not too late. You get to dream again.

Things happen. We make choices, which lead us to places we never thought we would be, dealing with consequences we never thought we would have to face. Yet here we are. While it would be easy to beat yourself up with the negative *"What if?"* questions or the *"Why did I?"* questions, those won't serve you as much as the *"What am I going to do now?"* question or the *"What do I want to do now?"* question.

Perhaps you didn't walk away from your dreams. Perhaps you're just in a place in your life where you achieved all the dreams you had and you're wondering, what's next? Or perhaps you stopped asking what's next all together and you're just getting through the days.

Maybe you've faced a tragedy and you feel like your dream was stolen or like you lost your ability to dream. Regardless where you may find yourself, you get to dream again – *if you want to*.

You get to choose how you want to move forward. You get to decide to stay down or to get back up. You get to go back to the drawing board and figure it out or to decide it's not worth it. Regardless what you decide, *you* get to decide and *you* must decide.

LETTING GO OF WHAT COULD HAVE BEEN

When track runner Derek Redmond was a teen, his dream was to be a record breaking Olympic Gold Medalist. He trained hard and was well on his way. During the 1992 Olympic Games, after winning his quarter-final, he was running in the semifinals when, a short distance from the finish line, his hamstring snapped causing him to fall to the ground in excruciating pain. When the stretcher-bearers came to take him off the field, he refused to go with them because he wanted to finish his race. As he was limping along the track, his father got past security and helped him finish the race. They later learned that injury ended his career as a professional runner.

Dreams don't die; however, sometimes they do. It may sound contradictory, but it isn't. There are times when the dream you've been working towards is no longer an option in the form you were pursuing; however, the dream to fully live out your God-given purpose never dies.

Derek's dream of becoming an Olympic Gold medal track runner died on the field that day, but the dream to be great stayed very much alive. He could have given up, but instead, he became a part of the Great Britain national basketball team and reached division 1 in the Great Britain rugby team. According to Wikipedia, he now serves as Director of Development for sprints and hurdles for UK Athletics and also works as a motivational speaker.

Derek's refusal to give up is what positioned him to be an **extraordinary failure***, *someone who stepped out and attempted something that they did not get; but* *something even greater than they imagined happened because they did not give up.*

FORGIVING ME

Part of moving forward, is learning to let go. **Part of letting go is learning to forgive.** When we think of forgiveness, we usually think about someone who wronged us or someone we wronged and often miss the less obvious piece of the puzzle, forgiving ourselves.

For a long time, I was so angry and I could not figure out why until I realized that part of what was holding me back was my anger and disappointment in myself. I made some choices and investments that lead to a lot of frustration. I allowed fear and people's opinion to keep me from taking so many chances and pursuing ideas that I had. I allowed insecurity to keep me in a perpetual state of planning and over-planning and perfecting the plan, and as a result, years went by with little impact. Since I allowed these things, there was no one to be mad at but myself. I had to get to a place where I accepted that no matter how bad I want to, I cannot turn back the hands of time and undo or redo some of the choices I made. I had to also get to a place where I realized I did the best I could with where I was what I had and what I knew.

You're going to make choices that you're not always happy with or proud of and choices that don't work out the way you plan. Though you won't be able to rewind, you do have options.

1. **FORGIVE YOURSELF**. Forgive yourself for all the wouldas, couldas, and shouldas.

2. **RECOGNIZE THAT YOU ARE STILL ALIVE.** Since you're still breathing, you can make new choices, which can lead to new realities for you.

3. **ACKNOWLEDGE YOURSELF FOR ALL THAT YOU HAVE BEEN ABLE TO ACCOMPLISH THUS FAR.** Make time to celebrate and acknowledge yourself for what you did right.

4. **RECOGNIZE AND ACKNOWLEDGE THAT YOU ARE FARTHER ALONG THAN YOU THINK YOU ARE.** Everything that you've gone through and learned along the way won't be wasted, and if leveraged properly, they can propel you further than you would have been without them.

5. **START WHERE YOU ARE.** This is a journey where you perfect along the way and not one where you must be perfect to get on your way, so decide to start right where you are.

A NEW BEGINNING

A second chance is just that, a second chance, a reset, an opportunity for a new beginning. If you truly accept the second chance, then the choices of your past and people's opinion can no longer define you. Don't allow what you think you should do or want keep you tied to an old dream. Seize your second chance and either go after an old dream or dream a new dream.

HOW TO DREAM A NEW DREAM

> **dream**
> to imagine that you can be, do, have, or create something that exists first in your heart and mind only and that may defy your present circumstances

1. **MOURN WHAT COULD HAVE BEEN.** Give yourself permission to experience your emotions.

2. **BURY THE OLD DREAM.** Let go of what could have been and put to rest how you thought the dream was going to happen. Let go of the time, money and resources you invested.

3. **FORGIVE.** Forgive yourself and everyone who may have contributed to the death of your dream.

4. **KNOW THAT IT IS NOT OVER**. It may look different than you originally imagined, but different can be better.

5. **DREAM A NEW DREAM.** Just because the initial dream may no longer be an option, it does not mean that a variation of that dream isn't still possible. What are the alternatives?

6. **SAY YES MORE.** Say yes to new experiences and things you wouldn't normally consider. Surround yourself with dreamers and people who are excited about life and passionate about what they're doing.

7. **EMBRACE THE TEMPORARY.** Do something for now. You don't have to make a life decision. If there's something that excites you now, then explore it now.

8. **DON'T GET STUCK IN THE TEMPORARY.** Give yourself a time frame. When your time is up, decide if you want to continue down this path or explore a new one.

9. **SUPPORT ANOTHER DREAMER.** While you are deciding what your next step may be, support someone else in making their dreams a reality.

10. **HAVE FUN.** Relax and just have fun.

SOMETIMES THE BIGGEST CHALLENGE IS SAYING YES TO PURSING YOUR DREAMS IN THE MIDST OF ALL THE REASONS YOU COULD SAY NO.

IT TAKES COURAGE
THE COST OF YES

REALITY CHECKUP

For the sake of realizing your dreams, are you willing to:

	YES	NO
Invest your time, energy and resources?	☐	☐
Do things you that may terrify you?	☐	☐
Say yes to things you don't feel prepared for?	☐	☐
Risk failure?	☐	☐
Give up the safety of the familiar?	☐	☐
Admit you need help and ask for it?	☐	☐
Separate from friends?	☐	☐
Be judged and misunderstood?	☐	☐
Keep moving forward even if everyone around you thinks that you should stop?	☐	☐

Between the doubts in your mind and the objections of others, you don't have to search hard to find reasons to not pursue your dreams. The question is, *in the midst of all the possible reason you could say no, will you dare to pursue the dream you dare to dream? And will you do so unapologetically?*

One of the main reasons why the word "dreamer" has such a negative connotation is because while many people are willing to talk about what we want, too few are willing to take action.

Our lives are not scripts we live out, but a series of choices we make that create a collection of experiences that we choose, whether actively, *with a decisive yes or no*, or by default, *making no choice and simply letting "whatever happens happen"*. The greatest things in life though, are not defaults; they're active choices. If you're going to be successful, you have to choose to be successful. If you're going to live fully, you have to choose to live fully. If your dreams are going to become a reality, you have to choose to say yes to pursuing them.

Like with most potentially life-changing decisions, deciding whether or not to go after your dreams, can feel like you're in a game of tug-of-war with faith, *the underdog*, versus fear, *the bully*. Fear will present so many valid objections and challenges, which can lead to **decision paralysis***, *the inability to make a decision because of crippling fear or an overwhelming number of options*. To avoid making a wrong choice you make no choice forgetting that you can't move forward standing still and that if you stand still long enough, you will start going backward. On top of that, you'll become a roadblock for others connected to you and your choices.

THE POWER OF WHY

Choosing to pursue your dreams comes at a cost. Beyond the financials, it will require an investment of your time, energy and resources. All of our journeys are different but regardless where you're starting or what your dream is, **you have to be willing to give up some things today for what you want and for who and where you want to be tomorrow.**

When I got my masters degree, my mom had certain expectations for me, and a well-paying nine-to-five job was one of them. My decision to launch a campaign, where I would be traveling across the country speaking and interviewing women, was not part of her plans. Truth be told, they weren't part of mine either, but pursuing your dreams will change things. It can disrupt your norm and put you in a place where you are constantly uncomfortable and being stretched. That's why your **why***, *the motivation and driving force that compels you to pursue your dreams,* is so important.

In the midst of all the changes that will take place, it's your *why* that helps you stay focus and that reminds you that what you're going through is worth it. Without a clear *why* you may start to resent the sacrifices, be envious of others, and even rebel against all the demands one day.

THE EVOLUTION OF YOUR WHY

There are the reasons we start things and the reasons we continue. When I started pursuing the *I Dare to Dream Project*, while it was always about women empowerment, I really just wanted to travel and to have conversations with CEOs and entrepreneurs. However, along the way, I started interacting with students and women of all ages and receiving messages about how something I said or did was leading them to pick up their music again, become authors, and go after abandoned dreams. Suddenly the potential impact of this project became very real to me and I was challenged to revisit my *why* and my dream.

If this whole campaign was just about a road trip with a catchy phrase, then I missed something. Because regardless how long it was taking, the road trip will happen and within a matter of months of it will be over. Then what? What was the purpose? What was it that I was hoping to accomplish? What impact was I hoping to have?

After really taking some time apart to reflect and to do some soul searching, I realized that as exciting as the campaign will be, it's just a means to an end. Ultimately the reason I'm doing this, the reason I'm willing to invest years of my time, energy and resources, the reason I'm willing to risk failure and separation from friends, the reason I'm willing to be judged and misunderstood is because I want to create a league of extraordinary purpose-driven women of standards, success and service. Women who are daring to pursue their dreams unapologetically, own their extraordinary, and have fun along the way. Women who never settle.

Why the *I Dare to Dream Project*? Because I believe in dreams. I believe they matter. And I believe that through the pursuit of our dreams, we embark on a journey of self-discovery where we find purpose and direction, which impacts the choices we make, including who we let in to our lives. We also develop a sense of self-worth and confidence that comes from finding our voice, standing for what we want and believe, setting and accomplishing goals and genuinely falling in love with the person we are and the person we're becoming.

So when things aren't going the way I want or when the journey starts taking longer than I expect, the vision of what's possible, the reality of how lives can be impacted is the why that mandates me to say yes and to keep saying yes.

When your *why* changes, not only will that impact your approach, it will cause the dream itself to evolve. In fact, **the clearer your why is, the clearer your dream and your approach will become**.

I used to think the reason we give up or say no to our dreams is because of fear. Now, I see we give up on our dreams because we don't realize the significance and the impact potential of what we're pursuing. *What is the why behind your dream? What is that compels you to say yes? How will it impact your life and the lives of others?*

IT TAKES COURAGE

When it comes to daring to dream and pursue, you are required to say yes knowing there are no guarantees. Sometimes you'll get what you want, sometimes the dream will die, and depending on what you are aiming for, sometimes the dream may cost you your life.

Some world changers, such as Martin Luther King, died because of their dreams and without ever seeing their dreams realized in their lifetime. At age 15, Malala Yousafzai, a Pakistani activist for female education and the youngest-ever Nobel Prize recipient, nearly lost her life when she was shot in the face because of her dream to see girls empowered through education.

Not all dreams will require that kind of sacrifice, but If your dream did, would you still say yes?

Saying yes takes courage and faith rooted in God, yourself, your dream, and others. It takes courage to be willing to go where those in your circle haven't gone before and to do what most are afraid of doing. It takes courage to say yes when doing so requires you to come face to face with fears such as how will your pursuits impact your relationships.

One of the costs of saying yes is a smaller entourage. There are a few people your dream will require you to distance yourself from and there are others who will walk away or distance themselves from you. If you're married or in a relationship, your yes can change the dynamics of that relationship, for better or for worse – that will be up to you and your partner to decide. But change is inevitable because you will change as a result of the journey.

KEEP OUT OF REACH OF CHILDREN

Those who are single face their own challenges. I remember I used to pray that I would meet my husband before I became recognized as a "success". I thought the more I did and accomplished, the less approachable men would find me and the harder it would be to find a mate. To prevent that, I decided to hold back. I held back the release of books, I held back sharing my dreams and I self-sabotaged. Fortunately, after some serious reality checks, I came to several realizations which shifted my perspective.

I was reminded that "**life waits for no one, not even 'the one'**". *If I placed my dreams on hold waiting for this man, how long would I be waiting? Plus, if I did meet him and I couldn't trust him with my hopes and dreams, then how could I trust him with my life and all of me?*

Since I generally process through analogies, I started thinking about medicine and how all the labels say "keep out of reach of children". The pharmaceutical companies understand that because of a lack of understanding of potential dangers, children wouldn't know how to effectively handle medicine.

In my desire to be "approachable", I was essentially positioning myself to be within reach of those who may not know how to handle me and all that I stand for. I realized that the right man for me is worth the wait. Even if it means that part of the cost of my yes is singleness for a season, he's still worth the wait.

Every dream does not require the same sacrifice, but whatever yours require, will you say yes? *Will you dare to challenge the status quo? Will you dare to step out of the ordinary? Will you dare to believe that something other than what you have experienced so far is possible for you?* It takes a lot to dare to pursue your dreams and one of those things is courage.

NOW WHAT

CREATE A VISION BOARD OF YOUR WHY.
Create a vision board of your *WHY* to remind yourself of why you said yes to your dream.

WHAT DO YOU DARE TO DREAM? #shareyours.
Record and upload a short video sharing what you dare to dream at **idaretodreamproject.com**.

HOW TO OVERCOME DECISION PARALYSIS

> **decision paralysis**
> the inability to make a decision because of crippling fear or an overwhelming number of options

1. Be aware of your deadlines and options.
2. Gather as much information as you can.
3. Know how this decision moves you towards your goal.
4. Trust your instinct.
5. Pick one or pick none – just make a decision.
6. Understand that there is a window of opportunity, so make a decision in a timely manner.
7. Understand that you will not always get it right, but it doesn't mean that you won't reach your goal.
8. Understand that you can course-correct.
9. Understand that you will not always have all the information in advance, yet you still must decide.
10. Understand that whether you get it right or wrong, it's all a part of the journey.

GREATNESS DOES NOT JUST HAPPEN. IT **IS A**N ACTIVE **CHOICE** THAT GOES BEYOND RESTING ON YOUR TALENT AND ABILITIES.

OWN YOUR EXTRAORDINARY
GO FOR GREAT

Growing up school came easy for me. Without putting in much effort, I was always an honor student, not the best, but among the best. It wasn't until my eighth grade graduation, as I watched the same students get called time and time again for actually being the best in their subjects, did I start to realize what complacency and laziness caused me to miss out on. I was good, but I wasn't great. Not because I couldn't be, but because I didn't choose to be.

It's one thing to make a decision to do something. It's another thing entirely to make a decision to go for great. **Greatness does not just happen.** It's an active choice that goes beyond resting on your talent and abilities. It requires you to be correctable, be unquenchable, and to own your extraordinary.

BE CORRECTABLE

Your ability to be great and to excel in all aspects of your life is directly proportional to your ability to receive and implement feedback. You have to be correctable and people have to be able to tell you the truth without fear of repercussions. It's not always easy because our emotions get involved and we can see it as an attack, instead of what it really is, a growth opportunity.

Two months before I originally planned to release this book, I got feedback on my manuscript, which really shook my confidence and honestly frustrated me. I may have mentioned this before, but I am extremely proud of this book. I believed in it so much that I refused to work with anyone who was not as excited as I was or who couldn't see or catch my vision. That's one of the reasons that instead of going with the publisher who was interested, I decided to start my own publishing company, *Unapologetic Press*, to release my books and the books of others who are seeking to expand their brand or message with a book. It's also the main reason that I chose to do the interior layout of this book myself.

That's why I was so taken aback when my god-sister Sam told me she couldn't get past the first few pages of the book, even though she tried. She said she felt no connection to me as the author and that she didn't understand the purpose behind the book. I was flabbergasted. As you can imagine, it wasn't easy to just sit there without trying to defend my work.

With feedback, we always have a choice – to either dismiss what's being said or to actually listen. I chose to listen and I am so grateful I did. Her feedback forced me to look at the manuscript again and to go deeper and answer questions such as:

- Who am I and why should readers care about what I have to say about pursuing dreams?
- Does a dream even matter?
- Are dreams for everyone?
- What real life examples can I give?
- How can I make the message more personal?

The book you now hold in your hands is the result of that conversation. Because I took heed of what she had to say, my message got stronger and clearer; the book went from 107 chapters to less than 35 and from ten sections to four; even the title changed from *Birth Your Dream: The Dreamer's Manual* to *Dare to Dream; A Dreamer's Manifesto*.

Feedback does not always equal truth, but if you learn to listen and check it for truth before you decide to take it or leave it, it can be the difference between success and failure.

Do you dare to be great? If so, be correctable.

BE UNQUENCHABLE

Part of why greatness is so beautiful and so celebrated is because of the commitment, dedication, focus, and hunger that it takes to get there. You have to be unquenchable. In other words, you have to:

- Refuse to be satisfied with less than your best,
- Refuse to be deterred by doubts and fears,
- Refuse to be stopped or silenced by failure,
- Refuse to get stuck in the temporary,
- Refuse to allow circumstances or people to pollute your mind, faith, and dreams.

To be unquenchable is the possession of a no-matter-what attitude and a laser focus that makes the only option success. When you choose to go for great, you are choosing to be a trailblazer and to go places that many are not willing to go because of the kind of investment required. You won't always be alone, but you have to be willing to go though none go with you, if that is what's required. While you may not always be able to go with those you know or grew up with, you will meet other trailblazers along the way who will become friends, advisors and sometimes even a spouse.

Do you dare to be great? If so, be unquenchable.

OWN YOUR EXTRAORDINARY

Another crucial ingredient when it comes to going for great is owning your extraordinary, recognizing your core genius and contribution and not apologizing for your talents and gifts, for your accomplishments, and for what you want and have. It's about being at a place where you don't need validation from others and you are not swayed by their lack of approval or by their praises. You accept that you cannot please everyone and that people's opinion of you has more to do with where they are and how they feel about themselves, than it does with anything you've done or could ever do. To own your extraordinary is to choose to pursue the dreams and desires of your heart unapologetically, holding nothing back. In short, it's an internal confidence that radiates and permeates through all that you do.

Do you dare to be great? If so, own your extraordinary.

At this point in my life, I can only imagine what it feels like to reach the end of a goal and know that I gave everything I had. I can only imagine what it feels like to have no regrets and to not have to wonder what would have happened if I tried harder? I can only imagine the indescribable pride that comes from knowing that I did exactly what I set out to do and exceeded my expectations. I can only imagine the meaning behind the tears I would cry when I reach the top of that summit because only I truly knew the price I paid in order to stand where I was standing.

I can only imagine these things because if I'm truly being honest with myself, up until this point, I had never truly gone for great. Don't misunderstand. I have accomplished great things that I am incredibly proud of. I'm just aware that there were many times when I held back and I refuse to continue doing that. Because it's not too late to be great, I'm going for it and I invite you to join me.

If you want what everyone else has, then go ahead and do what everyone else does. If you want what few people have, then do what few people are willing to do. If you want what no one else has ever gotten, you have to be willing to go and do what no one else has ever done. **I challenge you. I dare you. I implore you. Go for great.**

HOW TO MAINTAIN A STANDARD OF EXCELLENCE

> **standard of excellence**
> a decision to go for great

1. Decide to be your best.
2. Take the necessary actions.
3. Learn from the best.
4. Do what you say you'll do.
5. Finish what you start.
6. Address issues immediately.
7. Stay humble.
8. Stay grateful.
9. Give back to others.
10. Be patient with yourself.

THERE IS NO CURE FOR THIS
A PART OF THE PROCESS

Have you ever really wanted something? Hoped for it, prayed about it, sought it out, and then you got it? When my friend found out she was pregnant with her first child, she was ecstatic. This was what she waited for and it was finally happening. That's why I was confused when she told me how miserable she was.

While she was excited about the baby, she did not anticipate the toll the symptoms would take on her and how much her life was going to change before the baby even arrived. She didn't anticipate being unable to work and being placed on bed rest from her first trimester. And she certainly didn't anticipate dealing with morning sickness well into her third trimester and having to undergo major surgery that could have compromised the life of her baby.

Symptoms*, *challenges and changes along the journey of the pursuit*, are an unavoidable part of the process. We know challenges will come, but when they do, they can take us by surprise and tempt us to **abort*** the dream, *to say no or to walk away.*

MY SECRET SHAME

One of the things I didn't anticipate when I said yes to my dream, was the financial challenges I would have to face along the way. While I was traveling across the country and internationally, selling books, doing keynotes, presenting workshops and attending conferences, I looked really good on the outside, but I was drowning on paper. In between sessions I was dodging calls from debt collectors. When I got home from my trips, it wasn't fan mail waiting for me. It was letters from creditors and debt consolidation companies telling me that I qualified for their services.

That was actually how I found out how bad things had gotten with my finances. I suspected for a while that I was in debt, but I was so scared of the number that I never checked, requested a credit report, or tallied how much money I actually owned. One day I got a little orange postcard telling me that I qualified for debt reduction. When I saw the amount, I literally felt my heart drop. There is no way it could have gotten that bad! Oh, but it did.

Allow me to back track a bit.

After graduate school, I decided to become a full-time entrepreneur instead of getting a traditional nine-to-five job. One of the last jobs I had was at a government agency dealing with taxes. I only worked there three days a week, but I remember getting depressed every Sunday night and hating going to sleep because it meant that once I woke up I would have to go back to "that place." There was nothing wrong with the job. The people were nice. The pay was great. The environment was laid back. I didn't have to do much. And yet, I hated it. It was at that point I decided that it would never be enough for me to pursue a career path just for money. I had to chase my passion and trust that the finances would follow.

I don't know if I would still choose to not get at least a part-time job while pursuing my dream because of how stressful things got financially. However, at the time, choosing to focus on my dream full-time was what felt right for me.

It was also an easy decision to make because I was living at home with my mom, had $0 debt, no loans, a healthy saving account, and a credit score in the high 700s. I was always very mindful of my finances and always paid my credit card statements in full and on time. I was so determined to avoid debt that I chose to transfer out of New York University (NYU) my junior year of college and to complete my degree at Lehman College, rather than take a loan.

Unfortunately, in the beginning I was a bit delusional and had no idea how much it would cost and what would be required for me to realize my dreams. I also had no background in business and a lot of insecurities about my abilities to succeed in this new world. As a result, I invested thousands in trainings and seminars.

With every purchase I made I thought, *this will be the one that makes the difference; this will be the one that leads to my breakthrough*. While there were always some benefits, the main thing those purchases led to was debt, a bad credit score, and cat-and-mouse relationship with creditors and debt collectors. All because I didn't think I was enough and felt like I needed more information to compensate. In actuality, what I really needed was more implementation, accountability and confidence in myself and what I had to offer.

If you keep taking out of the same source and not replenishing it, what you have will eventually run out, which is exactly what happened to me. I started falling behind and was unable to keep up with all the bills and minimum payments. Every time I paid a bill, another was due. Plus, there were fees for insufficient funds, late payment fees, and interest charges. I felt slammed.

When I realized I was in trouble, instead of turning to my mom or anyone for help, I just tried to deal with things on my own. I was so ashamed because I spent all this time and money with little financial return to show for it. I was the one who told my mom that she didn't have to worry because I was going to be a successful entrepreneur and buy her a house that she would own free and clear. How could I now turn to her for help? If only I just went to her instead of assuming and allowing my emotions and feelings to carry me away.

I felt like giving up. I was mad and frustrated with myself and, truth be told, also with God because He gave me this dream, which, as far as I was concerned, was the reason I was having all these problems. On top of everything, my friends and loved ones would make comments like, *"Valerie, you're so cheap."* They didn't understand that every time I went out with them, it meant I was that much deeper in debt. *"Valerie, when are you going to get a job?"* They didn't know I was already beating myself up about whether or not I made the right decision in choosing not to work a traditional job. *"Valerie, you're single because no guy wants a girl who doesn't work,"* which made me think, then he really isn't going to want one with debt. I doubted myself, my choices and my self-esteem was taking a nosedive to join my finances.

WHEN HOPE HURTS

What do you do when you have a dream that compels you to pursue it, yet in spite of your best efforts you don't produce any where near the results you were anticipating? What do you do when you're judged and misunderstood by those closest to you? How do you deal with the disappointment and still choose to continue to pursue? What do you do when hope hurts? If you're Valerie, you pray and cry and pray and cry, then you write a book as you pray and cry.

Perhaps you're a dreamer who finds yourself under distress. You have this dream that you believe in and are making progress with, yet you're still contemplating aborting the dream, because in the midst of the pursuit, you find yourself dealing with incredible life pressures - stress, disappointments, discouragement, health crisis, financial crisis, relationship crisis, family crisis. All of which threatens both the pursuit of your dreams and you.

Where do you run when you start losing your passion and enthusiasm for the pursuit, and when you feel life flowing out of your dreams? What do you do when you call on others, in need of support or a word of encouragement or someone to just listen and no one's available?

Some call their coach or mentors, which is good; others call on their friends or family, which is also good; but I've learned to run back to God. There are certain points you get to where you don't need to hear from people first. Instead, you need to unplug from everyone and reconnect to God and your inner voice. Then, after taking a personal time out and checking in with yourself and revisiting your dream for yourself, check in with others.

TEAR EQUITY

Dreaming in the face of unrealized hopes and disappointments is unbearable at times, but the challenge is to still believe when throwing up your hands in surrender seems so much more appealing. **You have to learn to press on while facing every doubt, fear and insecurity, which are uprooted and constantly thrown in your face by you, by others, and by your results.**

There will be moments when you are disappointed and hurt and simply want to cry. When those moments come, you need to be okay with not being okay. Whether it's for a few minutes, a couple of days or even a few weeks. Allow yourself a safe space and outlet where you can experience your emotions without any judgment. Otherwise, the emotional build up may manifest as attitude, anger, bitterness and rudeness. It may leave you saying or needing to say I'm sorry.

As challenging as it can be, the process is not meant to take you out; it's meant to strengthen you and to test your commitment to follow through. With each teardrop you endure, your resolve gets stronger, the fire burns brighter and the dreamer inside of you is fueled by the moment of decision and clarity that often follows. During and after those tearful moments you will be forced to ask and answer the hard questions:

- Do you still want this?
- Do you still believe in what you're doing?

- Do you still believe that this is possible for you?
- Do you still believe that the dream is worth it?
- Are you willing to risk failure time and time again in order to realize it?

The decision to pursue your dream is not a one-time yes; it's a series of continuous yeses. You have to say yes daily and sometimes several times a day.

As long as your answers to those questions are yes, then keep moving forward. If not, then go find your yes. No matter what you face, make up your mind that you will not give up.

The road to success is paved with tears. So cry if you need to cry. Just remember that your tears are not signs of weakness, they are just a part of the process.

NOW WHAT

FOOD FOR THOUGHT.
How do you deal with disappointment?

What keeps you moving forward and saying yes to your dreams in the moments when you're tempted to quit?

Who makes up your support team?

BUILD A SUPPORT NETWORK.
If you don't already have a network of support, start putting together your own dream team of supporters, who will cheer you on and encourage you along the way.

WHAT DO YOU DARE TO DREAM? #shareyours.
Record and upload a short video sharing what you dare to dream at **idaretodreamproject.com**.

YOU ARE NOT IN THIS ALONE
ESSENTIAL CONNECTIONS

Pursuing your dream requires that you say yes before anyone else does and even if no one else does. At the same time, it's not a journey that you can do on your own. Even if you're independent, it doesn't change the fact that you need to be connected. Connections are how we learn and grow, give and receive. Four essential connections you need to maintain as you pursue your dreams are the connections with God, with yourself, with your dream, and with others.

CONNECTION WITH GOD

The connection with God is often overlooked because it's spiritual and intangible and often confused with organized religion, when, truly, it's about relationship. **It's based less on what we can see and more on what we believe.**

Had it not been for my faith and connection with God, I never would have made it this far. While I had people who believed in me and who saw my potential, those closest to me, those whose voices were loudest in my ears, were the ones telling me to get a "real job" and to basically stop wasting my time. Their intentions were well-meaning, but discouraging nonetheless. It was my relationship and friendship with God that sustained and continues to inspire and propel me forward. It ensures me that I can do all things through Christ, that I never walk alone, that I am Divinely-guided and protected, that all things are working together for my good, that everything I need will be provided, that there is strength in my weaknesses and that what I started I will finish.

Without a doubt faith is necessary. The question then becomes, *faith in what?* It's a question we must all answer for ourselves. *What is the source of your faith? What is it that lets you know that what you want and what you're going after is possible for you? What is it that lets you know that you can do this?*

The stronger your faith, the more stable and resilient you will be.

CONNECTION WITH YOURSELF

As much as the journey is about your pursuit, it's also about you. The same way you took the time to define your dream, you have to take the time to really look at and answer the questions – who do you want to be and who does your dream require you to be and become? Even if you think you already know the answers, embark on a journey of self-discovery and question everything.

Challenge the limiting beliefs you have about yourself. Challenge what you think is possible for you and what you think you're capable of. Challenge the things you once accepted as true that no longer serves you. **Explore the boundaries of every restriction and limitation that you've placed on yourself and that others placed on you, with and without your permission.** And do so without compromising your integrity.

The only way to do that is to venture out, which is exactly what the pursuit will challenge you to do. As you're defining who you want to be, intentionally choose to be that person. Not when your dream happens, but now.

CONNECTION WITH YOUR DREAM

A life coach once asked me, what does a speaker do? Without skipping a beat, I responded, "They market themselves, connect with others, invest in trainings, and prepare talks." The coach just looked at me and said, "Speakers speak."

As I was working toward being an effective, highly-sought-after motivational speaker and trainer, I was so caught up with taking courses and branding that I rarely did the thing that I said I wanted to do – speak!

Because it's possible to neglect the dream while you're working *on* the dream, you have to find ways to actively do the things you dream of doing, even if you can't do it to the scale you want to do it yet. If you want to be a speaker, speak. If you want to be a singer, sing. If you want to be an author, write. If you want to be an artist, create. You see where I'm going. Do the thing(s) you dream of doing now and figure the rest out as you go.

CONNECTION WITH OTHERS

People need people. Period. We need each other. What makes the journey of life so beautiful is the people we get to share it with. That's why being a part of a support community is so important.

People pay hundreds and thousands of dollars to attend seminars and to join masterminds and coaching groups because there's something incredibly powerful and synergetic about being a part of a supportive community of like-minded people connected through a shared experience, who understands you.

A support group is:

- A gathering of friends who may not have otherwise met,
- A place where you can go for understanding, support, feedback and guidance,
- A place to simply be without pretense or feeling the need to "fake it",
- A place where you can share your victories and be celebrated, share your frustrations and be listened to, share your disappointments and be comforted and encouraged, and share your challenges and questions and be guided,
- A place of connection where you just fit.

A support group is so important that if you can't find one you really connect with, then you should start one. Part of the vision for the @idaretodreamproject is to have both an online and offline community of fun, fearless, purpose-driven women. A community encouraging, supporting, challenging and celebrating each other. A community where we get to be there for each other.

For me, it's less about the number of followers and more about a truly engaged and supportive network, where we can live up to what a support group is meant to be. So join us. Send me a direct message, either via

Facebook or Instagram, introducing yourself and sharing what your dream is and what your journey has been so far. Share whatever you choose, I just want to get to know you and know how I can best support you.

As you maintain your essential connections with God, with yourself, with your dreams, and with others, the speed and magnitude of your success and impact will increase exponentially. Neglect any one of those connections and you will lose the benefits that can only come from that connection. Make these connections a priority.

NOW WHAT

CHECK YOUR CONNECTIONS.
Which of the following connections do you need to strengthen?

- ❏ Connection to God.
  Who/What do you believe in beyond yourself?
- ❏ Connection with Yourself.
  Create a vision board of who you want to be
- ❏ Connection with Your Dreams.
  Schedule time daily/weekly to do the thing that you dream of doing. Actually put it in your calendar.
- ❏ Connection with Others.
  Connect with @IDaretoDreamProject online

  If you don't already have a network of support, start exploring what your options are.

WHAT DO YOU DARE TO DREAM? #**shareyours**.
Record and upload a short video sharing what you dare to dream at **idaretodreamproject.com**.

IN THE SPACE BETWEEN YOUR EXPECTATIONS AND WHEN THINGS ACTUALLY HAPPEN, **YOU HAVE A CHOICE** – TO SEE IT AS AN OPPORTUNITY OR TO ALLOW IT TO STRESS YOU OUT.

THE TIME FACTOR
ANY MINUTE NOW

Have you ever looked outside and without having to check the forecast you knew it was going to rain? Whether it was because of the clouds or something in the air, you just felt it?

In a similar way, as you're getting closer to realizing your dreams, there will be this knowing inside of you that what you've been working towards is about to happen, any minute now. You will enter into such a state of flow. Things will start lining up for you. You'll get ideas that will help you overcome challenges you're facing and answers to questions you have. There will be such a sense of urgency that the temptation will be to rush to the finish line. However, you did not go through all of the ups and downs to finish hastily or half-hazard.

Timing is crucial in this phase. Your ability to patiently wait for the right time for every step you take will directly correlate with your level and degree of success. **Doing the right thing at the wrong time can be just as detrimental as doing the wrong thing at any time.**

THE TIME FACTOR

When it comes to dreams, timing is often relative. You'll set expectations, but then deadlines will change, setbacks will occur, life will present challenges, mistakes will happen and lessons will be learned, all of which impacts your time frame and can cause a considerable amount of stress. On top of that, those who don't understand what the pursuit takes may put unnecessary pressure on you to "hurry up" or to "just finish already".

In the space between your expectations and when things actually happen, you have a choice – to see it as an opportunity or to allow it to stress you out. There are two main ways that we stress ourselves out during this process, which can lead to us making a premature or delayed move:

1 **A PREOCCUPATION WITH TIME.** Along the way, many of us manage to get into a negative relationship with time. We live in constant fear that we're running out of it or falling behind. While it's important you're mindful of time, you must also understand delays happen and that they can work in your favor and position you in a better place than you would have been without them.

2 **A PREOCCUPATION WITH PEOPLE.** Because we're constantly plugged in, it's hard to not notice the success of others. It's equally hard to not compare. It's one thing if you're comparing for growth or inspiration, but all too often we use comparison as an opportunity to beat ourselves up, which will only end up sabotaging our own progress and success.

NECESSARY PAINS

While it's important to not launch prematurely, you also have to ensure that you don't allow fear or feelings of inadequacy, manifested in the form of perfectionism or procrastination, to delay you. Hours will turn into days, days into weeks and weeks into *"Maybe I should wait until next year."* That's why it's important to set a cut-off date and to remember that done is better than perfect.

To ensure we don't get complacent or take too long, we'll often get **contractions***, *life's way of giving you the push you need to take the next step.* They're caused by a combination of internal factors - *restlessness, dissatisfaction, a sense of urgency* – and external factors – *financial and relational challenges* – working together to usher you to the next level and to position you to birth your dream. It's similar to an eagle pushing its eaglets out of the nest when it's time for them to fly.

Contractions are often painful and uncomfortable, but they're also beneficial because pain pushes you to give birth to what is inside of you. It's the pressure that often wakes us up and forces us to make some much needed changes and decisions.

TEMPORARY RELIEF

As beneficial as it is, pain is also distracting, which is why we have the option of **epidurals***, *temporary solutions that you put in place to help you deal with some of the bigger frustrations of the final phases of the journey so that you can concentrate on execution.* While they don't stop the challenges that you're facing, they can release you to focus on action.

Some of the more common pains that dreamers experience includes financial stress, people pressure, and deadlines. If you are on the verge of your launch and you find yourself in a financial crisis – your funds may be depleted or you didn't get or make the money you thought you were going to – there are temporary solutions that you can put in place, such as getting a loan or a sponsor, renegotiating an agreement, asking for support, or getting a temporary job. If the people around you aren't providing you with the support you need and you decide you need some space, you can consider options such as housesitting. If you're struggling with deadlines, you may consider getting an intern or hiring someone who will support you on either a temporary or permanent basis.

Regardless what pain you're experiencing, know that there are options available to help minimize the pressure. If things start getting critical, then drastic measures may be required.

DRASTIC MEASURES

There are times when you play by the conventional rules, do everything that you know to do and nothing happens. The calls never come. The breaks never come. The opportunities you have been waiting for never come. Nothing. You may get some results, but nothing close to what you were anticipating.

In those moments you have to ask yourself, *"How far are you willing to go to make your dreams a reality?" Are you just going to simply allow the dream to die or keep postponing it, or are you going to make a way?* Depending on your dream, that may mean you self-publish, put on your own gallery show, or organize your own concert where you are the main singer.

Three instances when **drastic measures***, out-of-the-box, *unconventional approaches to overcoming challenges you are facing so that you can get the results that you're after*, are required include the following:

1 **BREECH LAUNCH**, *when a launch is complicated by poor sequencing and wrong positioning*. There will be times that you have to launch from a non-ideal place because of:
    - Good intentions, but bad advice,
    - Following what worked for someone else thinking, it would work for you, but it didn't,
    - Lack of information and research,
    - Moving so fast that you missed crucial steps.

    You can still complete your process, but often with challenges and stress that could have been avoided had you made more strategic decisions. Depending on how far along you are in the process, there may be time to reposition yourself to make the launch easier.

2 **LAUNCH OF MULTIPLES**, *when one idea leads to unexpected dreams and spinoffs*. Don't be surprised if and when your decision to pursue one dream leads to other projects you didn't anticipate.

    This book was never part of my initial plans. In 2011, after my first couple of interviews where women were sharing such intimate details of their stories, I decided to share my own story. What started out as a script for a five-minute video lead to me writing and publishing my first book, *I Am Beautiful: Finding the Confidence to Pursue My Dreams*. That book in turn led to me becoming a motivational speaker and trainer.

In 2013, while searching for answers and a way to keep my dream alive, I started journaling my thoughts and questions. That search and writing resulted in this book, *Dare to Dream: A Dreamer's Manifesto*. While writing *Dare to Dream*, I researched pregnancy looking for correlations with dreams. Since people would constantly refer to their dream as their baby, I wanted to know how pregnancy and child-birth could help with the dream-birthing process. That question lead to another book project, *Your Dream Is Your Baby: What to Expect When You're Expecting a Dream*. For a preview just check out *Dreamer's Dictionary* at **idaretodreamproject.com**.

I also noticed there were many correlations with faith-based principles. What started out as side notes and personal devotions, turned into *God Is My Business Coach: The Dreamer's Manual*.

In addition, I saw and experienced how big of a factor fear was and how much it hinders us. After sharing my concerns with a friend, she challenged me to write a breakup letter to fear. That exercise became the catalyst for the *Dear Fear, It's Over* campaign, which includes a compilation book with *101 breakup letters to fear*. You can be a part of the book by writing and submitting your own breakup letters to fear. Learn more at **idaretodreamproject.com/dearfear**

You see how one idea can turn into multiples?

3 **COMPLICATIONED LAUNCH**, *when there are challenges from the onset you have to overcome or when things don't go as planned.* While a breeched launch occurs because of choices made, a complicated launch has to do with the reality of the circumstances you find yourself in. Depending on where you're starting and what your goals are, you might have some specific difficulties to overcome. However, with some simple out-of-the-box thinking, you can find ways around or over those roadblocks.

One of the ways I'm overcoming my challenges is by learning to just ask. It's a simple concept and may seem obvious, yet it's so underutilized because of our fears and the stories we have around asking. If there's something you need, reach out to those around you and give them an opportunity to support you. **Do not underestimate the power of an ask.**

KEEP IT SUPER SIMPLE

There was an 18-wheel truck that got stuck while trying to go through a tunnel. After unsuccessfully trying to get out, police, firefighters, experts and engineers were brought in to figure out how to get the truck unstuck, but every attempt that was made failed. A kid observing the scene turned to his dad and said, "*Why don't they just let the air out of the tires?*"

When faced with challenges, we can over-complicate the process and miss the obvious. I, for one, was extremely guilty of this, which is why whenever I feel overwhelmed or stuck on a project, I take a step back and ask myself, *how can I K.I.S.S. this?* In other words, *how can I simplify and keep things super simple to accomplish the goal?*

That's what drastic measures are about, asking yourself what will it take for you to make your dreams a reality while taking into account the challenges that you must deal with. It's about the **push***, *a no-matter-what decision that you're going to go all the way and that you'll find a way*. It's about completion and involves an element of desperation that leaves no room for excuses and pushes you to the point where you're no longer concerned about many of the things that stopped you in the past.

This journey is not a race where you have to finish first or fast, but it's about you doing what you have to do, when you have to do it, as best as you can do it, so that you can finish. **Be patient with yourself**. Allow things to take as long as they need to take. Just be very mindful of how you manage your time. Otherwise, you may be left feeling extremely overwhelmed, which can lead to a state of constipation.

NOW WHAT

FOOD FOR THOUGHT.
What is your relationship with time?
What causes feelings of stress and anxiety when it comes to time?
What are some of the frustrations and challenges that you're currently experiencing?
What requests can you make to overcome those challenges?
How can you KISS the process and your dream?

JOURNAL OF IDEAS.
Time to pull out your journal of ideas. Make note of any ideas that come to you that will help you overcome challenges you're facing. Don't judge your ideas. Record them.

OUR NATURAL NEED TO GO TO THE BATHROOM TEACHES US A LOT ABOUT **PRIORITIES**.

DEALING WITH OVERWHELM
THE STATE OF CONSTIPATION

Our natural need to go to the bathroom teaches us a lot about priorities. You can try to hold it in, put it out of your mind, or dance it away, but when you "gotta go", you "gotta go". And if you don't go and allow things to get critical, you won't be able to concentrate, you will start getting weak in your knees, and in spite of your best efforts, things might come out on their own. Since no one wants to put on a show of that nature, you learn very quickly how to put everything on hold and excuse yourself, so that you can relieve yourself.

We need to apply that same principle and sense of urgency when it comes to life outside of the bathroom. There are things that are important and things that are pressing. In order to properly function and give the important things the attention they require, you have to learn to attend to the **pressing things***, *the things consuming your mind and demanding your attention*.

When I started working on this book, it was not the best time, at all. I was completing the Anniversary edition of my first book, working on websites, and preparing for workshops and speaking engagements. Plus, I'm a team of one, which means I also had to deal with the day-to-day stuff, the legal and copyright stuff, the financial and branding stuff, the social and fitness stuff (because sanity breaks are a must), and the other stuff that people want you to help them with.

What do you do first when so many things and people are demanding your attention? The most pressing stuff. How do you know which is the most pressing? Learn to listen.

- What is consuming your mind right now?
- What do you keep coming back to?
- What do you keep thinking about when you should be working on something else?

For me, in the midst of everything I had to do, I had a pressing need to complete this book. It meant delaying projects and engagements and completely unplugging for months at a time, but I had to finish. It didn't make sense at the time and it honestly seemed backward and may have even cost me some relationships, but I could not concentrate and be present for anything else until I got this out. It was only as I got closer to completion did I start to see why it was so pressing to write this book. **Focusing on the pressing simplified the important**. The writing and editing process was crucial in helping me get the clarity I needed for everything, from my branding to the websites to my long-term vision for what I wanted to create. In the end, I would've been so far behind if I didn't follow the pressing urge to complete *Dare to Dream*.

STATE OF FLOW

Finding the balance between the pressing and the important and trying to do everything when it needs to be done can be overwhelming. As you look at your life, you will start to realize that you're either in a state of flow, a state of the runs or a state of constipation.

The **state of flow*** is *rhythmic progress accompanied by a sense of peace and an inner knowing that you are right where you're supposed to be.* You're setting goals, meeting deadlines, producing tangible results, stretching yourself, but not taking on too much. There's no straining and minimal pushing is necessary. Even if there are moments when a push is required, it usually comes in the end and allows for the completion of the process.

Being in flow means that you're aware of the time; you're in the right position; you're open and relaxed; and you're willing to let go, which includes knowing when to let go of money, people, places and things. It also includes knowing when to release certain products and aspects of your projects.

STATE OF THE RUNS

Too much flow and you may find yourself in a **state of the runs***, *when you release or attempt to do too much, which results in stress and overwhelm for yourself and others.* Part of the challenge with the state of the runs is what you release, you must maintain. And without a system in place, it can cause you unnecessary stress and to be out of balance.

The state of the runs is often experienced in the beginning of the journey (caused by over excitement, lack of experience and knowledge about the process) and towards the end of the journey (cause by an over excitement, eagerness and impatience). Other causes include:

1. **AN OVERWHELMING FLOW OF IDEAS.** We get all types of ideas – from average to good to great ones. The danger lies in the inability to distinguish between the three and the attempt to execute them all, and all at once.

2. **PROGRESS AND ENCOURAGEMENT.** The closer you are to launching, the more excited you get and the more you want to do. You're so in flow that the temptation is to go fast and release everything that you've been working on.

3. **INSECURITY AND LACK OF FEEDBACK.** When you're not getting the feedback you need or want, it can lead to insecurities and may cause you to launch projects and ideas prematurely in order to get the response or reaction you desire.

4. **COMPARING YOURSELF TO OTHERS.** Instead of focusing on your own goals and strategies, you try to do everything you see others doing.

One thing you need to remember is that it's not about quantity. It truly is about well invested time in developing the great ideas into exceptional quality ideas. If you're in the runs, then make the time to take inventory and to identify the great ideas and the ideas you need to let go of.

STATE OF CONSTIPATION

Anyone who has ever experienced physical constipation knows that it is painful. You're backed up, uncomfortable, agitated. You know you have to go; you want to go; at the same time, you're afraid to go, because you also know, it's probably going to hurt.

The **state of constipation*** is no different. It is *frustration and overwhelm brought on by a lack of progress, completion and results*. You're backed up on deadlines, projects, and promises. You're on edge and having trouble concentrating. There's so much to do, yet you don't know where to start. If left unaddressed, the state of constipation can cripple your progress, hinder your ability to move forward and make you a toxic, negative person.

Some of the more common causes of the state of constipation include fear, incompletes, too many voices and opinions, and over-commitment. The following is a list of additional possible causes:

1   **I.G.S. – INFORMATION GATHERING SYNDROME.** Obsessive information gathering that delays action and progress, which usually stems from feelings of inadequacy, and can lead to decision paralysis due to an overwhelming amount of options.

2   **SHADE OF BLUE SYNDROME.** An obsession over minute and sometimes-insignificant details, which can be fixed down the line, that delays progress.

3   **COMPARISITIS.** Negatively comparing yourself to others, which can lead to insecurity, low self-esteem, lack of motivation and competition where you're either putting someone else down to feel better about yourself or you're putting yourself down.

4   **DISEASE TO PLEASE.** A desperate desire to fit in and be accepted to the point where you make decisions based on whether or not others would approve, even if it compromises the goals you're working toward. It's also known as **the shoula*** because of *the constant overwhelming need to do what you or someone else feels you should be doing, even if it conflicts with what you want or need to be doing.*

5   **IMITATIONITIS.** Trying to be something or someone you're not. It's usually a result of admiring someone or something to the point you try to copy, even when it's not authentic to who you really are.

6   **CRISSCROSS MINDSET.** Driven by material wealth instead of purpose. You start confusing **success***, *the fulfilling of your God-given purpose*, with the outcomes of success, which include but are not limited to money, influence, impact, legacy, certain freedom and luxuries, a certain lifestyle, etc.

7   **SELF-CRITISM AND JUDGEMENT.** The way you speak to yourself is demoralizing and paralyzing and makes you blind to your accomplishments. It makes you susceptible to other's feedbacks and criticisms, compromises objectivity and robs you of confidence.

As you look over the list, notice that most of the causes have to do with mindset and actions or lack there of. If you learn to monitor and manage your thoughts and to take the right actions at the right time, you'll be able to establish and maintain a state of flow. Being organized and having a system will also help you facilitate flow. Just beware of **mylanta moments***, *quick fixes which lead to temporary relief without necessarily solving the problem*. There are times you need to put a bandage on things; just remember to actually go back and address the root issues.

HOW TO GET BACK TO A STATE OF FLOW

> **state of flow**
> rhythmic progress accompanied by an overflowing sense of peace and an inner knowing that you are right where you are supposed to be

1. **TAKE INVENTORY.** What are the pressing things that are demanding your attention right now and that if you complete will have the biggest impact in moving you forward?

2. **SORT AND COMPLETE.** Go through what you need to do and sort out what needs to be completed, deleted, outsourced, or filed away for the future.

3. **K.I.S.S. YOUR DREAMS.** Keep It Super Simple. Look for ways to simplify what you're currently working on.

4. **BREAK OLD PROMISES.** If there are things you said yes to but you now realize you cannot honor, reach out to the respective people and let them know. Take responsibility. Be honest. Apologize. Move forward. In the future, delay making promises you cannot and do not want to keep.

5. **SAY NO.** You are going to have to say no to opportunities that seem great and to people who will not always understand. It is what it is.

6. **ASK, ASK, ASK.** Ask for the support and resources you need. You won't always get a yes, but at least give people an opportunity to say yes.

7. **CREATE SYSTEMS AND CHECKLISTS.** It's easier for people to help you, if you know what you need and you give clear instructions.

8. **CREATE A CHEER SQUAD.** Making time to actually celebrate your progress can be the biggest game shifter for you. Who are the people you can regularly connect with who will cheer you on by celebrating your work and encouraging you during your missteps?

9. **STEP AWAY.** Take time out for you. Take a break, unplug, go on a vacation, and then come back with a fresh perspective.

10. **GET LOVE. GIVE LOVE.** When you feel loved, do something fun, or just enjoy a nice meal in good company, oxytocin, *the hormone of love*, is released, which balances cortisone, *the stress hormone*. You will also get the same benefits when you give love to others. So get love and give love.

DON'T SACRIFICE YOURSELF AND **YOUR DREAM** BECAUSE YOU DON'T WANT TO OFFEND SOMEONE.

ONLY A SELECT FEW
BEHIND CLOSED DOORS

Can you hold my hand as I push?
As exciting as this is, I'm in a lot of pain.
There are a lot of tears and complications may arise.
I'm frustrated and making a mess of things.
I'm overwhelmed; emotional and suddenly overcome with fear and doubt in my ability to do this.
In between the pressures and the demands, I'm worrying about the future.
I guarantee you, I will say things that don't really sound like me.
I may get an attitude.
I may talk crazy and seem unreasonable and overly sensitive.
I don't mean to make excuses, but I'm scared.
In the midst of all that I just want to know, can you hold my hand as I push?
Are you willing to stand by my side even if it causes you pain?
Are you prepared to talk me through my doubts and my fears?
Will you tell me how great I'm doing and encourage me to keep moving forward?
Can you stand by my side and be silent with me?

Do you promise not to judge me and throw my shortcomings in my face?
Will you help me remember that I can do this and that it's possible?
Can you hold my hand as I push?
Can You Hold My Hands, Valerie Jeannis, 2014

Having a dream and deciding to pursue that dream is so exciting. The possibilities, the people you meet along the way, the celebrations, the things you learn - it's amazing. At the same time, it can also be very challenging.

On July 4, 1952, Florence Chadwick was on her way to becoming the first woman to swim the Catalina Channel. On her way to the shore, she fought and swam her way through dense fog, freezing cold, and sharks. The difficulty was that every time she looked through her goggles, all she could see was the dense fog. After swimming through all those obstacles, she reached a point where she decided to quit only to learn that she was only a half a mile from the coast. She gave up, not because she was unable to go the distance, but because she couldn't see the end goal through the fog. She later said, "I'm not making excuses. If only I had seen the land, I could have made it." Two months later, she went back and swam the Catalina Channel again. This time, in spite of the bad weather, she was so focused that not only did she accomplish her goal, but she beat the men's record by two hours!

You will never want to quit more than when you are closest to the finish line. That's when everything will seem too hard and when you'll suddenly feel as through you cannot go another step or take another hurdle or setback. You can get so worn out by the process that you have **blurred faith***, the *momentary loss of faith which makes it hard to see that it's possible for you to get from where you are to where you want and are called to be.* It can be caused by doubt, fear, a lack of perceived progress and success, or just exhaustion. Your faith in the possibility will return, especially with progress, encouragement and increased success. **Your challenge, to believe and maintain your faith, not simply because of what you see, but often in spite of it.** In those moments it's important that you have people you can turn to, who will help you keep hope alive.

A SELECT FEW

Whether you're just launching a phase of the project or the project in its entirety, it's essential that you are surrounded with the right people. Just like with a woman in labor, everyone in your inner circle should be selected because they're willing and able to help you work toward your ultimate goal, the successful launch of your dream.

Prepare yourself for the fact that there are some people who will be offended because they were not chosen. They will even try to make you feel guilty, selfish, or ungrateful for leaving them on the outs. But it's not about them. It's about you. And yes, perhaps it does require you to be a little selfish, but for the sake of your dream, be selfish for a little while. Don't sacrifice yourself and your dream because you're afraid of offending someone.

There are three primary groups of people that you should ideally have around you when you're getting ready to push, launch.

1. **THE ENCOURAGER**, *the person holding your hands*. This is the person encouraging you, wiping your brows, and giving you their hand to squeeze. They can't do it for you, but what they can do, they go out of their way to do. Be kind and patient with them because while they're being there for you, they have their own lives and challenges as well. Thank them too much, because they are priceless.

2. **THE COACH**, *your mentor, advisor*. This person has gotten to know you in ways you don't even know yourself. Their job is to guide you, help you navigate any emergencies that come up, be honest with you and give you feedback, even when you don't want to hear it.

3. **THE ENFORCERS**, *the ones you hire, freelancers, contractors*. They execute orders and support you in getting what you need done.

It may take some time to find the right team members, so start building your team as soon as possible. Get recommendations. Make note of anyone you come across that you might want to work with. Above all, listen to your inner voice. Your dream matters and whoever stands beside you should believe in both you and your dream.

CUTTING THE CORD

In the movie, *Nanny McPhee*, when the nanny first meets the children, she tells them, *"There's something you should understand about the way I work. When you need me, but don't want me, then I must stay. When you want me, but no longer need me, then I have to go. It's rather sad really, but there it is."*

It can be rather sad, but it's a reality that we must all understand and come to accept – many of the people who are with us today on the journey and who play a role in where we are and in helping us launch, will not always be there. It's not because either one of you did anything wrong; it's just the way it is. We can try to fight it, but that doesn't change the facts or make it any less true. People often come into our lives for a purpose and once that purpose is fulfilled, they will continue on their journey as you continue on yours. Part of your growth is learning when to cut the cord and being able to do it with a spirit of gratitude and confidence that regardless of who is no longer a part of your journey, you will make it.

NOW WHAT

FOOD FOR THOUGHT.
Who holds your hands along this journey?

Who is your mentor?

Who are your enforcers?

Are there any cords you need to cut?

CREATE A FAITH-BOX TOOLKIT.
What are the tools, people, and resources that you can connect to during your moments of blurred faith?

For instance, my faith box toolkit includes letters, notes and cards with words of encouragement that others have given me or said to me

WHAT DO YOU DARE TO DREAM? #shareyours.
Record and upload a short video sharing what you dare to dream at **idaretodreamproject.com**.

NO MATTER WHAT
UNQUENCHABLE

My faith was tested
My health was challenged
But I learned God still healed
In the midst of the storm

My finances depleted
Debt threatened to overwhelm me
But I learned God still provides
In the midst of the storm

My dream was attacked
Its weaknesses exposed
But I learned God still covers
In the midst of the storm

The naysayers taunted me
The doubters accused me
But I learned God still justifies
In the midst of the storm

Trouble raged around me
Doubt raged within me
But I learned God still anchors
In the midst of the storm

And when the storm passed
And the waters calmed
They searched for me in the midst of the rubbles
But they did not find me there because
I am still standing after the storm
Still Standing, Valerie Jeannis, 2013

Throughout the entire journey a lot of emphasis is placed on the dream and rightfully so. However, beyond the dream, every yes you said, every challenge you faced, every time you fell and got back up – all of it was to give birth to you, the dreamer.

It is literally impossible to go through the process and not be changed, for better or worse. Either you get bitter or you get better. A bit cliché, but true nonetheless: bitter or better. Bitter because it took too long. Bitter because people didn't show up. Bitter because it's not what you thought. Or you get better. Better because you're stronger. Better because you're wiser. Better because you're able to help others on their journey.

Your confidence also increases. Each time you successfully completed a task, took a risk, chose to keep moving forward after disappointment, got positive feedback and recognition, your confidence increased. Though all the benefits are not always obvious, throughout the process, you have grown.

There are times when we think we just want to fast forward and jump right into success, but when you see how far you've come and how much you've learned, how can you not look back at it all and smile, perhaps even with gratitude?

DECIDING TO GO FOR IT ALL

As I look at the map of the United States spread across my wall and think about the *I Dare to Dream Project*, the "impossible" dream that started me on this journey, I renew my commitment to push and I say yes. Though I still have more questions than answers, I'm at peace with that because I know everything is going to work out.

When it's all said and done, I am just a girl who decided to go for it, daring others to do the same. I am stepping out on faith to prove that the impossible is possible, first to myself and then to every dreamer with a dream. Because I know the difference it can make, I decided to keep an open diary on the website, where I share the highs, lows, good, bad and other. My hope is that in doing so, it will remind you that you are not alone in your feelings or experiences. I also hope that as you follow my journey, you will share your own and get involved in the campaign.

YOU GOT THIS

We are in this together. I ask of you the same thing I ask of myself, to just go for it. In spite of how you feel, the magnitude of the task or how long it takes for you to figure it out, just go for it.

> ***So what if they think you're a delusional dreamer?*** *Just don't let it be true.*
> ***So what if they think you're wasting your time?*** *Just care less.*
> ***So what if you fail?*** *Just become an extraordinary failure.*

> ***So what if you don't have everything you need?*** *Just make a decision and watch provision follow.*
> ***So what if you get stuck sometimes?*** *Just take steps to get back in flow.*
> ***So what if they don't believe in you?*** *Just believe in yourself.*

This is your dream and your one life to live. You can play small or you can unapologetically dare to dream the dreams of your heart and then dare to pursue.

Refuse to allow where you are to limit the magnitude of your dream. Imagine that you can be, do, have or create something that exists first in your heart and mind only and that may defy what you could have ever believed was possible for you. And do it with no shame, no regret and no apology for wanting what you want. It's all possible. You just have to decide.

Regardless what happens or how long it takes, make up your mind that you are going all the way. You may stop or slow down for a little while. You may be hurt and cry sometimes, but no matter what, do not quit because **giving up is not an option.**

> All success starts out with an IDEA
> Turned into a DREAM
> Followed by a DECISION
> Built upon by ACTION
> Developed through THE PROCESS
> And brought to fruition by the PUSH
> **It Starts with a Dream, Valerie Jeannis**

NOW WHAT

DECIDE.
What you dare to dream?
Why do you dare to dream?
Do you dare to pursue?

JOIN THE INSTA-CLASS @DaretoDream_101

CONNECT WITH US ONLINE @IDaretoDreamProject

ENGAGE ON idaretodreamproject.com.

LEAVE A REVIEW.
I would love to hear from you. *What did you love? What are your take-aways? What are your dreams?* You can post your feedback on Amazon.com, send an email **hello@ValerieJeannis.com** or my favorite, send me mail at 55 West 116th Street, PO Box 360, New York, NY 10026. If you write it, I'll read it ☺

WHAT DO YOU DARE TO DREAM? #shareyours.
Record and upload a short video sharing what you dare to dream at **idaretodreamproject.com**.

APPENDIX

I CHALLENGE YOU TO TAKE THE TIME TO **SEND A PERSONALIZED THANK YOU** TO AT LEAST FIVE PEOPLE WHO HAVE BEEN THERE FOR YOU THROUGHOUT YOUR JOURNEY ...

THANK YOU TOO MUCH
ACKNOWLEDGEMENTS

TO MY MOM, WHOM I LOVE AND AM INDEBTED TO. From the beginning you sacrificed for me and stood up for me. These past five years you stood by me as I stepped out on faith and pursued my dreams. You didn't always understand the vision, but that never stopped you from supporting me. After God, you gave me my first yes and invested in both me and my dreams. You wiped tears from my eyes and hugged me through disappointments. You always made sure I ate and to ask if I was all right. I don't know how many people would accept the sometimes-unusual requests of a dreamer, but you did. For all that and so much more, I am beyond grateful. I love you for who you are. I love you for what you taught me. I just love you just because you're you and I wouldn't trade you for the world.

TO MY PASTOR, BISHOP CARLTON T. BROWN. Thank you for being a shepherd who was willing to take time away from the ninety-nine to listen and speak life to the one.

TO MY STEPDAD, EMMANUEL FLEURY. You don't speak much or ask a lot of questions, but you're always there and ready to give me advice when I ask. I love you and thank you for giving me the space I needed these past few years to pursue my dream.

TO NANA JOAN BYRD. Thank you for being my friend and mentor. Thank you for being honest with me and for listening to me, whether it was at Dunkin Donuts, at a restaurant, at the corner, at a bus stop, or on the phone. Thank you for challenging me to live the words I write. I love you all the time and appreciate you beyond words.

TO IFYTAYA DECK. There is a painting of praying hands that tells the story of friendship and sacrifice. When I think of you, I think of that painting. Thank you for standing in the gap with me. You challenged me, believed in me, yelled at me, refused to allow me to settle for less than God's best, and never judged me. Thank you for being one of my most faithful and consistent sources of encouragement, my friend, and my prayer partner.

TO PAULINE KERKHOFF. My friend, we have laughed together, cried together, and had cool new experiences together. With you I learned to laugh again on a journey where I spent so much time crying. Thank you for being that kind of friend. I look forward to celebrating the realization of our dreams during a gratitude walk in Japan and Joburg.

TO FRIENDS WHO GAVE ME BEAUTIFUL KEYCHAINS AND ALLOWED ME TEST DRIVE WEIRD NICKNAMES; TO FRIENDS WHO PATIENTLY LISTENED AS I TALKED THROUGH CHAPTER AFTER CHAPTER; TO FRIENDS WHO SAT IN THE CAR WITH ME AND DEBRIEFED AFTER MEETUPS AND SPEAKING ENGAGEMENTS; AND TO FRIENDS WHO PARTICIPATED IN TEXT MESSAGE SERMONS. I love and appreciate each and every one of you and I thank God for your friendships.

TO SAMANTHA ROSELINE PRINDILUS. I normally avoid mentioning family by name at all cost; however, how can I not acknowledge you? Your honest feedback about the manuscript challenged me to reevaluate and to take my own advice and go for great. This is a different book because you were honest with me. Now I seize this moment to challenge *you* to go for great as you venture into the world of being a children's book author.

TO CAROLL SCHWARTZ. Thank you for seeing something in me and for believing in the dreamer *and* the dream. You're an amazing life coach and your clients are blessed to have you in their corner. You can learn more at **coachyourdream.com**.

TO SEPTEMBER DOHRMAN. I have said it before and I will say it again, you will never know the difference you made when, for an hour, you stood by me as I literally unrolled my dream in front of you and proceeded to share in great detail. From the bottom of my heart thank you.

TO MY SISTER'S KEEPERS – ANN ANORJUSTE, KIMBERLY ANTOINE, TASHA BAPTISTE, SANDY BASTIEN, ERMANY BEAUBRUN, CHRISTINA BERNADIN, ANGELA CASTILLON, EMLYN CASTILLON, GINA CASTILLON, CELYNE DANIEL, CARLINE DANIEL, VANESSA DERAVIN, JESSICA LAPORTE, KESHIA LAPORTE, FARRAH MENARD, FRIDA PHILEMOND, FABIOLA VALCIN, JENNIFER VALCIN, ANDROMAQUE VILBRUN. Thank you for the fellowship. Whenever I speak, I always tell myself, *I'm just speaking to the girls.*

TO THE FOCUS GROUP AND REVIEWERS – ROSLYN ALLEN, ERMANY BEAUBRUN, REUBEN BEAUBRUN, SHANA BENNETT, FELICIA BLAISE, CARLA BROWN, EMMANUAL FLEURY, HOLLIS HEATH, RALPH JEANNIS, ENOCK JEAN JULIEN, PAULINE KERHKOFF, TAICHA MORIN, WILSON PAUL, SAMANTHA PRINDILUS, JENNIFER ROSENWALD, EBONY SMALL, CHIKE UKAEGBU, SANDY VALCIN, EILEEN WOODBURN. It's one thing to read a complete manuscript, it's another thing to read one in progress. Thank you for your willingness to take the time to read and critique my work. Your feedback was invaluable.

TO JENNIFER ROSENWALD & CLAUDINE WILLIAMS, MY UNOFFICIAL EDITORS. Both of your attention to detail and your notes and feedback were icing on the cake. Thank you so much for the time you amazing ladies invested and for sharing your love and enthusiasm for the English language with me.

TO ALL THOSE WHO WERE THERE FROM THE BEGINNING AND THOSE WHO WERE THERE FOR A SEASON. Whether it was a day or three years – IT MATTERED and for your time, words, encouragement and faith, thank you.

TO MY UNQUENCHABLE SELF. It wasn't easy, but look at what you did! I am beyond proud of you. Never say impossible again because already you've proven that the impossible is possible.

TO MY HEAVENLY FATHER AND FOREVER FRIEND, THE ALPHA AND OMEGA, THE BEGINNING AND THE END, TO GOD, MY BUSINESS COACH. I would have never thought that I would be grateful for all those who were unavailable and for the season of limited finances that I had, but I am. I am even more grateful that season is over and will never again return because I am moving out of its zip code. However, had it not been for the challenges and limitations, I would have turned to people or hired out whenever I had a question or needed something done. Instead, I learned to turn to You, which allowed me to get to know and appreciate You on a deeper level. I also learned to tap into what You placed inside of me. You have coached me through this *entire* process and gave me the strategies I needed to not only succeed, but to do so exceedingly and abundantly above all that I could have asked for or thought. Thank you for being my business coach and for trusting me with this dream.

It's hard to write these acknowledgements and not be overwhelmed with gratitude. It's funny, because there were so many times along the journey where I felt so alone and so forgotten, but looking back at this list and thinking about all the different people I could have easily added shows me once again how deceiving feelings can be. We are never truly alone, regardless what we feel. We just suffer from circumstantial amnesia.

As I close this section, I challenge you to take the time to send a personalized thank you to at least five people who have been there for *you* throughout your journey, whether they were there for a brief season or a lifetime. Even if they were a source of frustration to you, I challenge you to reach out to them and to genuinely say thank you for the role they played.

DREAMER'S DICTIONARY

TERMS	DEFINITIONS
ABORT A DREAM	To walk away or say no to the pursuit of your dream
ACCELERATORS	People with contagious faith that make you feel like you can do anything
ANCHORS	People who will see and point out potential pitfalls and dangers before they ever celebrate or cheer you on
BLURRED VISION	The momentary loss of faith which makes it hard to see that it is possible for you to get from where you are to where you want and are called to be
BREAK UP WITH FEAR	To make a choice and a declaration to no longer allow fear to hinder, cripple or stop you from pursuing your dreams or going after what you want
BREECH LAUNCH	When your launch or process is complicated by poor sequencing and wrong positioning
COMPARITIS	Constantly comparing yourself to others leading to unnecessary stress, insecurity, and delayed progress

TERMS	DEFINITIONS
CONCEPTION OF A DREAM	A process where something outside of you (an inspiration or idea) connects with something inside of you (a passion or your purpose) to form an idea in your mind that becomes a dream worth pursuing for you
CONTRACTIONS	Life's way of giving you the push you need to take the next step. The discomfort caused makes it impossible to remain complacent and pushes you to make decisions.
COST OF YES	The process you must go through in order to give birth to your dream and enjoy the fruit of your labor
CRISSCROSS MINDSET	Motivated by money instead of purpose and passion. Results from confusing success with the outcomes of success, which include but are not limited to money, influence, impact, legacy, certain freedoms luxuries and lifestyle, contentment, etc..
CYCLE OF QUITTING	Habit of aborting dreams and not following through on ideas
DARE TO DREAM	To give yourself permission to unapologetically pursue the dreams of your heart regardless of age, insecurities, current status or circumstances, or other's experiences and opinions

TERMS	DEFINITIONS
DELUSIONAL DREAMER	Someone with false or unrealistic beliefs and expectations about what it will take to make their dreams a reality
DISEASE TO PLEASE	The desire to fit in and be accepted, to the point where you make decisions based on whether or not others would approve, even if it compromises you and your goals
DREAM	A vision that you can be do have or create something that exists first in your heart and mind only; A bigger vision for your life that goes beyond your current reality
DRASTIC MEASURES	Out-of-the-box, unconventional approaches to overcoming challenges that you are currently facing so that you can get the results that you're after
DREAMING UNAPOLOGETIC ALLY	To refuse to allow where are to limit the magnitude of your dream
EPIDERAL	Temporary solutions that are put in place to help you dream with some of the bigger frustrations and distractions of the final phase of the journey so that you can concentrate on execution
EXTRAORDINARY FAILURE	Someone who stepped out and attempted something that they did not get, but something even greater than

TERMS	DEFINITIONS
	they imagined happened because they did not give up
FORGIVENESS	A decision to let go of the anger, bitterness, and resentment towards someone, some thing or yourself in spite of what you might feel, that is followed up with action
INFORMATION GATHERING SYNDROME	Constant delay of progress and action in search of more information and training; often stems from feelings of inadequacy
IMITATIONITIS	Decisions about what to do next are made based on what someone else is doing. You become a copycat and a knockoff
INNER VOICE	Your instinct or inner GPS, an inexplicable knowing
MULTIPLE LAUNCHES	When one idea leads to unexpected and unplanned dreams and spinoffs, which leads to a rapid succession of multiple releases
MYLANTA MOMENTS	Quick fixes that lead to moments of temporary relief, which do not necessarily solve the problem
OVERDUE LAUNCH	When the launch of what you are working on is delayed or being held up

TERMS	DEFINITIONS
OWN YOUR EXTRAORDINARY	A decision to unapologetically stand in your greatness; an internal confidence that permeates in all that you do
P TEST	A test of passion and purpose to help determine if an idea is or can develop into a dream worth pursuing for you
POWER OF CHOICE	The power to decide for yourself what you want in any given situation
PRESSING THINGS	The things consuming your mind and demanding your attention
PUSH	The height of the execution and action phase; Your no-matter what decision to keep going all the way to the finish line
RECKLESS BEHAVIOR	Activities you engage in to either help you feel or help you forget about the dream you gave up on
SHADE OF BLUE SYNDROME	Delayed progress caused by an over obsession and inability to make decisions about minute details, which can easily be corrected moving forward
THE SHOULDA	A constant overwhelming need to do what you or someone else feels that you should be doing, even if it conflicts with what you need to be doing
STATE OF CONSTIPATION	Frustration and overwhelm brought on by a lack of progress, completion/results

TERMS	DEFINITIONS
STATE OF FLOW	A rhythmic progress that is accompanied by a strong sense of peace and an inner knowing that you are right where you are supposed to be
STATE OF THE RUNS	When you release or attempt to do too much, which results in stress and overwhelm for yourself and others.
SYMPTOMS	Challenges and changes that are part of the journey of the pursuit of your dreams
TEAR EQUITY	Tears shed, often alone, as you fight to keep moving forward and to make your dreams a reality
UNQUENCHABLE	A refusal to be discouraged or talked out of your dream by refusing to be satisfied, subdued or to settle for less than
WHAT-IF SYNDROME	When your dreams become nightmares and you are constantly taunted by the dream you gave up on and you fantasize about what could have been; Regret
YOUR WHY	The motivation and driving force that compels you to pursue your dreams and makes it worth it to pay the cost of yes

> **CHECK OUT THE DREAMER'S DICTIONARY ONLINE**
> idaretodreamproject.com/DreamersDictionary

Introducing

#I DARE TO DREAM PROJECT

A CAMPAIGN DARING YOU TO PURSUE YOUR DREAMS UNAPOLOGETICALLY
www.IDaretoDreamProject.com

FOLLOW US ON @idaretodreamproject

A WOMAN ON A MISSION

idaretodreamproject.com @idaretodreamproject

AUTHOR AND MOTIVATIONAL SPEAKER VALERIE JEANNIS IS ON A MISSION TO DARE WOMEN AND YOUTH TO PURSUE THEIR DREAMS UNAPOLOGETICALLY

"I believe in dreams and ideas. I believe they matter. I believe they have the potential to change lives, impact generations and to change the world. And I believe that they are integral in our search for purpose, direction and self-worth.

Starting with me, I made a decision to stop aborting my dreams and ideas, to break up with fear and to just go for it. And I am on a mission to support and challenge others to do the same."

With a mandate to challenge women to never settle, author and motivational speaker, VALERIE JEANNIS is the creative force behind the *I Dare to Dream Project*, a campaign daring women to pursue their dreams *unapologetically*.

Her books include: *Dare to Dream*, *I Am Beautiful*, *Diary of a Dreamer*, *Your Dream Is Your Baby* (Spring 2017) and *God Is My Business Coach* (Spring 2017).

Valerie is also an international motivational speaker and rapidly becoming a highly sought-after voice to millennials, young professionals, and those in faith communities pursuing personal development, transformation and the discovery of purpose.

Valerie teaches and conducts workshops and lectures based on her books, the Dare to Dream philosophy, and her unconventional approaches to realizing the dream. Her interactive presentations and down-to-earth speaking style are just some of the reasons students themselves request her and administrators continuously bring her back.

To learn more about how to book Valerie for your next event or conference or how to order bulk copies of her books, visit **www.ValerieJeannis.com** or send an email to **Info@ValerieJeannis.com**.

NOTES